GW01417845

3 50
16/8

ONE LIFETIME

IS NOT ENOUGH

An Autobiography by Patrick Kelly

2

(Originally) Edited by Carmel Kelly

(First) Printed 1986

(2nd Ed) Joseph Farrell, 2002

Copyright © 2002 Joseph P. Farrell

Printed in the United States of America

Published by Glenock Publishing

Grand Junction, CO

Printed by Pyramid Printing

Grand Junction, CO

Cover Painting: Australian Gum Tree Leaves –

Mary Kelly Casey

Edithvale, Victoria, Australia

Please direct all inquiries and book orders to:

Glenock Publishing

Joseph P. Farrell

570 ½ A Villa St.

Grand Junction, CO 81504

ISBN 0-9721686-0-5

ONE LIFETIME IS NOT ENOUGH

GLENOCK PUBLISHING

DEDICATION

To my late wife, Daisy J. (Judy) Cloud Farrell, without her this book would not have been possible. "Always is Forever."

ACKNOWLEDGEMENTS:

I wish to acknowledge the valuable contribution of, William John Bradley, Janet Bullock, Mary Casey, Joyce Corneille, Gloria Heitsman and Tess Patton.

Thanks go to the Kelly Family members in Australia, Ireland and the United States, who encouraged me in the process of publishing this book.

Thanks also to, The Omagh Public Library,
St. Eugene's Catholic Church Rectory Staff, The Ulster American Folk Park Library and Research Center.

Table of Contents

BOOK ONE

THE EARLY YEARS

BOOK TWO

THE EMIGRATION – IMMIGRATION YEARS

BOOK THREE

THE ROMANCE YEARS

PREFACE

This journal may be a series of disjointed episodes. So be it. That is what it is, just the story of a boy growing up and the environment in which he was reared. It is possible that continual mention of Ireland may become boring but it may be interesting in so far that the Ireland of my youth does not exist in the conditions of those times.

I find it very difficult to use the appendage Northern Ireland to the part where I was reared. Certainly Tyrone is in the Northern location of the Island, but the term Northern Ireland denotes a separate State which is anathema to a vast number of Irish people; it represents a fragmented Ireland and the dream and ambition splendid is to see a free united Ireland. (Now don't put it away. There is a lot more, for which in time, I will give good reason.)

Ireland is dotted with places of historic interest. Tyrone was the stronghold of the O'Neill clan - remains of Harry Avery O'Neill's castle is on the outskirts of Newtown Stewart. In the town there is the walled remains of another castle built by an enterprising Scotsman, one Stewart, no relation to the royal Stuarts, though history has it that James II spent a night there before his ignominious departure for France. On the morning of the departure, he set fire to the castle which was then gutted. In my boyhood the walled courtyard was used as a hay and corn market. In my 1978 visit, a large supermarket was impinging on the site and vandals had been busy knocking off dressed cornerstones and stone mullions from the windows.

History also records that Newtown Stewart was razed by burning and rebuilt three times. The town is surrounded by beautiful and rich homes mostly owned by descendants of Scottish planters, while descendants of original inhabitants farm the poor hill country. A visitor to the district should not miss the beautiful valleys of Gortin and the Sperrin Mountains.

The Mourne River, which is an amalgam of several smaller rivers flows past the town on its way to joining the River Foyle at Lifford. Above the town is a hill or mount known as Bessy Bell; it was always my ambition as a boy to reach the top of Bessy Bell but I never did.

The Great Northern Railway, which traversed the Mourne Valley in my youth has been long abandoned and the rail station is derelict. One of the delights of going to town in my youthful years was to stand on the road arch over the railway and feel the blast from the steam engine as the train went through on its way to Derry or Omagh. A journey on the train was a rare experience.

My main excuse, if I need one, for including glimpses of my boyhood's countryside, is linked to my belief in the effects of environment on human development and behaviour. Each era, of course, has its particular effects on human behaviour; in our day the gap between country bred and city bred dwellers was wide, owing to the prevailing transport facilities or rather the lack of them. Today when the aim of every boy and girl on reaching maturity is to own a set of wheels and with the younger fry getting gratis transport, the gap narrowed. The best I ever managed was an old retired bicycle which more than often I carried home.

Cut off from the traps and pitfalls of town and city life, was to my mind a blessing for our family. I often wonder what may have been the outcome had Neal and Mary preferred to keep on living in Glasgow. On looking back I recall with nostalgia shopping nights when I was a small boy. Saturday night was pay night; it was also late night shopping. Mary Ann would wait until she saw Neal on his way home, then leaving the young ones with stern warnings we would head off through the fields to meet him and transfer the necessary finance to Mary Ann with which to replenish the larder for another week.

I expect today's mams might find this amusing. Yes, probably with their credit cards and credit accounts, etc. Well, Mary Ann could have got credit at any shop in town, but as she always said, "there's got to be a day of reckoning, and if you can't pay today there is no guarantee you will do any better next week." I inherited the philosophy and sometimes I think it has been an inhibition as far as investment has been concerned. It was a three mile walk into town but Saturday night shopping was always an event for me as a small boy. There was magic in the town, just plodding along over the new bridge with gaslights gleaming in the Mourne waters. There was always an acrid smell of coal smoke in the air, and happy bands of youngsters chasing along the street. Motor cars were rare, but there were always horse drawn vehicles spinning along...to a small boy from the country certainly a fairyland...to the grown up, one long main street with a few branching streets and alleys, dull, drab grey and quiet, and in 65 years it has not altered much.

Coming home at night, laden with groceries must have tested Mary Ann's endurance and my tiny legs would also feel the strain. I can recall one fine summer's night when we sat down to rest about halfway home. Here I suffered my first experience of disorientation. After resting and girding up our burdens I started off back to town. With strong persuasion from Mary Ann, I was turned around. It was a lonely mountain road and it was not until I saw the lights of home that I was convinced and regained my bearings.

Albeit all my memories of boyhood labour, the winter months would invariably bring several heavy snowstorms, work in the fields would then be hampered and there would be some let up for the younger fry. After school, and having ensured that a supply of potatoes and turf had been laid in, our occupation would be sliding on the frozen ponds or dashing down a snow covered hill on a toboggan or a sleigh. I made an advanced model and steel shod it. We could get a good speed downhill but there was one drawback: the sleigh had to be brought back to the top of the hill again. Here the girls came in handy, for a stand on the back of the sleigh on the down run we allowed the girls the honour of toting the machines back up to the top again. I wonder...male chauvinist PIGS...Ai Ai!

I wonder how many dear old grannies look back now and think of those happy days and recount to their grandchildren stories of hands blue with cold and knees and backsides skinned through falls and headers into the hard frozen snow!

"Oh for the days of the Kerry dancing, and the ring of the piper's tune. Oh for those hours of gladness, gone alas, like youth too soon."

* * * * * * *

So, having undertaken and completed a record of my life since travelling to Australia, the task is not so tedious as I thought it might be. I intend the journal as a record for future descendants.

~Patrick Kelly~

Preface to the Second Edition

I started in genealogy in 1995 because it sounded interesting and I wanted to find information about my wife's natural father who had died when she was young. I took a course at Mesa State College in Grand Junction, Colorado. The course was an introduction to PAF (Personal Ancestral File), the software program developed by the Church of Latter Day Saints (Mormon). The instructress was Mrs. Dorothy Roper, who's dedication to the teaching of the program inspired me. Subsequently I joined a group from the Museum of Western Colorado for a field trip to the LDS Library in Salt Lake City, Utah. On our first night a guest speaker lectured on the subject of finding lost ancestors who would have been of draft age, during the First World War.

I was able to locate the draft information for my wife's father, Fred Lee Cloud, and went on to build a database of her ancestors, tracing them back to the first William Cloud, who came to the United States with William Penn. Penn set aside five hundred acres of land for William Cloud, in what was to become Chester, Pennsylvania. My love left me in 1999 to join the Lord. For a while I could not seem to do any more genealogical research and put it aside. In the year 2001, my partner, Mrs. Gloria Heitsman, and I made a visit to Ireland, the land of my parent's birth.

I belonged to several Internet groups who had an interest in Co Tyrone, Ireland. In planning my visit I asked for advice about where to begin my research of my mother's family, the Kelly's, of which I had no knowledge. I had told the group of the townland where my mother was born. I received information about a book that had been written about the Townlands of Gallon (Gallon Upper, Gallon Lower, and Gallon Sessiagh) by an author named William John Bradley. I was able to locate John Bradley and talked to him by phone requesting a copy of his book. I owe a deep debt of gratitude to John, who arranged to meet and show us around the area. He introduced us to many of the people in the townland who knew my mother's family and we also found that a cousin (the existence of whom I knew nothing) was living in the very house where my mother and some of her siblings had been born!

Tess Patton, my cousin, (her grandfather was my mother's brother) opened her heart and her home to us. Tess also arranged for us to come one evening and there I met a sister, Claire and two of her brothers, Sandy and Danny. Present also was Rose McNamee McGrinder, one of Tess' cousins. We had a wonderful visit and it was there that I learned of another cousin, Patrick, who had immigrated to Australia in 1925. I was shown his autobiography and some poetry, which he had written, as well as letters, to Tess.

Tess' sister Claire had with her a copy of a family history chart which Patrick had sent to them. Claire was kind enough to give me the copy. Tess, in turn loaned me, Patrick's autobiography and his other writings so that they could be copied. I was so impressed with Patrick's autobiography that I contacted his family in Australia, and requested permission to publish his work. Patrick's children were kind enough to give me permission to publish his autobiography.

In order to get a better understanding of Patrick, it was decided that I should travel to Australia to obtain more information on his life and his family. In November of 2002, my companion and I traveled to Melbourne, Australia; here we met his children, Patricia, Mary, Claire, Neal, William (John) and Josephine and their families.

During our visits we walked in Patrick's footsteps through the countryside, towns and cities of Victoria, Australia as well as in the townlands of Co. Tyrone, Ireland. It is my desire that you as the reader will share in his experiences.

There may be historical and grammatical errors encountered as you read the book. The publisher made the decision to leave the book as Patrick wrote it with only minor corrections for spelling or punctuation. Diligent effort has been made to find the author of each poem in the book and where found the author has been credited with his work.

BOOK ONE
THE EARLY YEARS

BOOK ONE

Oh, Danny boy the pipes are calling,
From glen to glen, and down the mountainside.
The summer's gone, and all the roses falling,
It's you, it's you must go and I must bide.
But come ye back, when summer's in the meadow,
Or when the valley's hushed and white with snow.
It's I'll be there, in sunshine or in shadow,
Oh Danny boy, Oh Danny boy I love you so.

For the good are always merry,
Save by evil chance,
And the merry love to fiddle,
And the merry love to dance.

~W.B. Yeats~

CHAPTER ONE

On the fifteenth day of May 1902, two young people, Neal
Kelly and Mary Ann Quinn were married at St. Eugene's Catholic Church
in Glenock near Newtown Stewart, Co. Tyrone in what is now known as
Northern Ireland. Neal, who had been working in Scotland is listed as a
mason's labourer and Mary Ann's people were farmers, or to use a
sometimes derogative, [Neal's family] they were peasants. Whatever, there
was a little resentment on my mother's side because she married an
ordinary labourer. With hindsight, I can say no couple could have been
more devoted and no family could have had more faithful parents.

I, their first born, saw the light of day in the city of Glasgow,
Scotland on 13 August 1904. My dad had taken his bride back to Glasgow
where his work was. Both my parents were Irish; there was the belief that
the children of Irish parents did not thrive in Glasgow. On perusing the
history of the working and living conditions of those times, I am inclined
to believe that many Scots children did not survive either. So be it. At the
mature age of five weeks I was taken back to be reared in the pure air of
old Ireland.

From stories my father related, life in those times was not easy.
How happy one of our local seers could be at that statement. Students of
history will recall that the Boer War had not long finished; men who had
upset their lives to serve in the Army found themselves without a job. There

was also an upsurge of resentment at the conditions of work that existed and there was a continual struggle for a living wage. Trade unions were only shadows, they provided little protection. I could imagine young Neal battling in the squalor and misery that was Glasgow in the 1900's. One picture could be of interest to women fighting for equality today. Women were engaged in wheeling coal at the pit heads, and at the brick works wheeling barrow loads of bricks; boys were working in the coal mines. Women were popular with employers; they did a man's job for half the pay. Women's Liberation!???

There was a strike on the wharves. Employers retaliated by bringing in boatloads of coolies probably from Shanghai or Hong Kong.

My mother was a first class needle-woman which was considered a must for girls of her time. She put her skill to good use, and in all probability contributed more to the family budget than Neal did. Arising from her dress making ability Mary Ann made friends with two dear ladies who were also my unseen friends for years until they died at a very advanced age. They had what I suppose would be called a boutique; they supplied elaborate trousseaus and paid well for work done, and many years later when Mary Ann returned to Ireland she would still help out with rush orders. Misfortune hit these dear people in 1910. Farrows Bank, where most of their savings were deposited, closed its doors, causing unlimited misery!

I'm not sure of the date but my father also talked of the Tay Bridge disaster where a train crashed into the Tay. This journal is not intended to be a historical record, rather incidents and events are recorded to give some idea of the background of the boy growing up in the early 1900's.

Mary Ann's father [John Quinn] was still alive when she returned from Glasgow. Her mother [Nancy Morris Quinn] had died when she was young. My birth apparently healed the schism within the family. I never had a memory of my maternal grandfather. I think he died in my first or second year, but I was told he was very proud of the only grandchild he was to know. Mary Ann had one brother, uncle Jack, and a sister, Kate. With these dear people I had a second home.

My paternal grandfather Pat Kelly, and Grandma Rose were still alive. Old Pat, as we called him, lived to be a ripe old age. He was a stonemason. If you have ever taken time to look at some older buildings or bridges and marveled at the chiseled stonework, then say an Ave for those skilled people, the stonemasons, of such was old Pat. I was not mature enough to digest the interesting things he had to tell; he must have been over seventy at that time. Rose was his second wife. Four children by his previous marriage had gone to America, that Mecca of the Irish, as it was also the vampire that drained the best blood of Ireland. Pat and Rose had ten children, six boys and four girls; some I knew but others had either gone to America or were deceased. Indeed I have a fine harvest of cousins in the U.S.A.

Above is pictured the Roman Catholic Church of St. Mary's located in Sessiagh O'Neill in County Donegal. The plaque in the church has the location spelled as "SESSIAGHONEILL".

The church was built in 1828 and was renovated in 1988. It was in this church that Patrick's grandfather and grandmother, Patrick Kelly Sr. and Rose McMenamin Kelly were married on June 17, 1869.

Rose McMenamin was from Egglybane, County Donegal while Patrick Kelly Sr. was reported to be from Inishowen. There is no documentation for his birth location.

==

Pat came from neighbouring Donegal and got a small holding in Gallon near Newtown Stewart. My sister lives there now. Rose survived

Pat for several years. Strangely I never developed that affinity for or with Grandma Rose that I did with Pat. I know in lots of cases small boys have a deep affection for Grandma. In my case I think my mother's sister, Kate, after my mother, had my affection. I know my father had a deep caring for his mother and always visited her regularly. Of course she was getting old when I remember her but I've always held the memory of burnt porridge and over-salted stews. What I am trying to kindly say, she would have given the world's worst cooks a run for their money.

I recall grandma Rose sitting in her armchair with her little snuff box, a little pinch inhaled into her nostril, followed by a gusty sneeze. Snuff seems to have gone out of fashion now. I had a grand aunt who smoked a clay pipe. She must have been a liberated lady! I used to feel sometimes that there was a little snuff mixed up with Grandma Rose's scones.

Let me now pay tribute to Rosy. She was married very young and she reared ten children and I think lost two more. It could have been no easy job in the late 1800's. In these modern times with all modern conveniences two children seem to be a burden for some parents. During her lifetime there were three major wars, and there must have been extreme hardships. And it's to her credit that she raised a family of good honest upright citizens who have in turn done honour to her and to Pat.

This is a typical stone bridge found in Ireland. Patrick Kelly Sr.
(Patrick's grandfather) was a stonemason. He may very well have
worked on this bridge south of Omagh.

CHAPTER TWO

When memory is allowed to run rampant it is inevitable that chronological sequence will suffer, so in order to give some coherence to this chronicle, some regimentation of the faculties will be necessary. Perhaps here I should make some apology for grammatical shortcomings, which may occur.

When Neal and Mary Ann arrived back in Ireland in the winter of 1904 prospects for raising their family must have been grim. I have often wondered why Neal did not join some other members of his family in the U.S. One logical answer was that Neal was primarily a man of the land; perhaps the quiet fields of Ireland held more appeal than the city jungles in the U.S.A. Had finances been available there is no doubt that Mary Ann and Neal would have been good farmers.

With his knowledge of farm work, Neal soon found a job as ploughman, which was recognized as a first class farm job. The wage by today's standard was a shocker, 10 shillings a week and meals. The hours of work were from 6 a.m. to 6 p.m., six days a week and four hours every third or fourth Sunday, according to how many permanent hands were employed. Mary Ann, like the good farmer she was, supplemented the meagre wage by keeping poultry and a few pigs. Many times in the coming years the supply of boots and clothing for little bodies would be dependent on when the hens started to lay, so naturally the hens were treated with a lot of respect.

In retrospect I believe my childhood was a happy one. I did suffer from a sort of guilt in loneliness, which increased, as I grew older. This is something, which I find hard to define, just restlessness and a longing to see what lay beyond the next mountain. I hated the winter when visions of the horizon were limited. Maybe it was all part of a normal boy's growing up. Schooldays were good and I tried to make the most of the opportunities afforded by our little country school with a staff of two teachers. My teacher was diligent beyond the demands of duty. He had been educated for the priesthood and besides our secular training he managed to impart the fundamentals of our spiritual needs; his examples have remained with me through life. Mary Ann and Neal were perfect examples in this respect also. It takes a firm faith to get up on a Sunday in winter and struggle through a blinding blizzard three miles to Mass.

This was the Gallon School. There was a school in Gallon for one hundred fifty years. This building was opened in 1870. John Kelly was the first principal having been appointed to the original school in 1856.

William John Bradley of Gallon Sessiagh was the last principal of Gallon School, serving from 1967 until the school closed in 1969.
For more on the Gallon School it is recommended that the reader obtain a copy of William John Bradley's book, GALLON, *The history of three townlands in County Tyrone from the earliest times to the present day.*

John has gathered a great many details on the school and the pupils who attended. It is a must for genealogical research in this area of County Tyrone. The book can be ordered from:

Mr. W. J. Bradley
7 Cloncool Park,
Culmore, Derry BT48 NS
e-mail: wj.Bradley@uafp.co.uk

My father's family were a very temperate people though it was known that old Pat had been an expert in producing the living water, or poteen as it was known. The story went that he never disposed of any of his product locally, but I can recall many tales of his exploits and escapes from the excise men. Dodging the bailiff and the excise man was apparently a national past time for Granddad's generation, and from all accounts from his early years old Pat was a man's man.

It is universally recognized that the Irish are a gentle, kind and courteous people. I believe it was St. Patrick who told them: "Go forth and teach all Nations." Mind you, in the course of Evangelism it may have been necessary to use a little extra persuasion with a shillelagh, which was a well polished blackthorn cudgel. As my Uncle Jack told me, there is no better inducement for man to see reason than a smart tap on the cranium. He may not have used those exact words but when Jack Quinn finished an argument his opponent was left in no doubt as to what he meant.

As I have stated my mother's home (the home of my mother's childhood) was always open to me and I took much advice from my Uncle Jack Quinn (my mother's brother). One example I did not follow. I have and had, an abhorrence of alcohol; that was Jack's failing; he was a good farmer but he spent a lot of time in the Pub. Market and Fair days were a bit of a nightmare and many times as a boy I would bring Jack and several boozy companions home in the farm cart. Meantime my dear Aunt Kate would be doing the milking and farm chores. Let it not be thought that I was just an onlooker on the farm. I can't ever remember being without some chore to do. And there was always a full work season; there was spud planting, turnip hoeing, turf cutting and drying, then there was the hay and oat harvests and spud digging. There was always a job for a willing small boy. Then there was minding cattle on the common land before and after school, and if the urgency of the job meant missing school, then so be it, and to hell with the truancy man.

Unlike the children of our mercenary age, there was little monetary reward, a good meal, yes, and maybe a pair of boots at Christmas. Maybe it would surprise, but from the day I started work at twelve years old (I mean steady work for a wage) I never handled a penny of my wages; being the oldest my money went to support the family. There were six in our family, three boys and three girls. One girl, Rose, died at fifteen months. "Pocket money," well, that I got by doing jobs outside ordinary working hours which were from 6 a.m. to 6 p.m. at seven shillings and six pence (37 pence in modern money) for a six day work week with additional hours every third or fourth Sunday. I was a keen soccer player and on many a heart-breaking occasion I had to yield my place in the team because it was my Sunday to work. Those, my children, were the good old days, but we were happy. We had no need of drugs or sneaking around burning our lungs out with tobacco, and alcohol was taboo. I only saw my father sick with alcohol once, and that was when some smart idiot laced his soft drink with brandy.

I was only a toddler when Uncle Jack dosed me with raw whiskey, to cure a bad cold he said; I nearly died, and the relationship between Mary Ann and Jack was very cold for some time. They say there is nothing to make some Irishmen mad as the sight of an empty whisky bottle. I know the name Kelly has a very honoured (?) place in Australian history. One of the clan was highly elevated by the Government. ₁ The name, translated from the Gaelic means "fighting man." Whether this is an honourable connotation or not I don't know. Could it be that they are just ordinary tavern brawlers? I chose to think of my ancestors the *O'Ceallaigh*, as adorned in shining armour with beautiful polished shillelaghs, poised in a breach of a hawthorn hedge with stacks of dead whisky bottles behind them. By the way, our coat of arms, Crest, is a round tower, etc. Motto - the Lord is a tower of strength unto me.

₁ Ed. note: a notorious highwayman Ned Kelly was hanged but his name is still honoured in some parts of Australia.

The portal tomb is often better known by the name *portal dolmen* or, more simply, *dolmen.* The portal tomb in the picture is located at the Ulster History Park.

The tripod portal dolmen is, for many people, the classic image of a megalithic tomb and that at Legananny, County Down, is probably the best known in Northern Ireland; in the Republic of Ireland, the best known is undoubtedly, Poulnabrone in County Clare.

Surprisingly, perhaps, the portal tomb is the least numerous type of megalithic tomb in Ireland – only 175 are known. They are mainly distributed across the northern part of Ireland although there are some 35 in the southeast of the country and a few in County Clare and south County Galway.

The portal tomb consists of a single, smallish chamber, usually narrowing toward the rear, having an entry at the eastern end between two large portal stones set inside the line of the side stones. It is covered by a single huge capstone that often rests on the portal stones and the back stone and slopes down toward the back of the chamber. In many instances the side stones have disappeared, leaving only the portal stones, back stone and cap stone – the tripod dolmen with which we are familiar.

Both cremated and inhumed remains have been found in the small number of portal tombs that have been excavated, although there is no clear indication of which was the preferred rite of disposition. The portal tombs may date to the early – to mid fourth millennium B.C. [c, 4000 – 3500 B.C.]

(Text and photo, by Permission of the Ulster History Park)

CHAPTER THREE

I was still a small boy in a man's world, not quite eight years old when on the 10th of April 1912 a large new ship left England on a maiden voyage to America. Aboard were hundreds of young Irish people bound for America.

"It was on the 10th April the Titanic did set sail
With many a brave young Irish heart from green robed Innisfail,
Who meant to shun vile tyranny, and foul oppression's sway,
To labour for a livelihood, a thousand miles away."

Many of the Irish were from Derry and Donegal, among them some of my father's friends. Also aboard were many rich tourists enjoying a royal time. According to the reports of the day, champagne and caviar were the order of the day in the dining rooms. On the 12th day of April, two days out from England the reputed unsinkable ship struck an iceberg and sank.

"In other lands the grief is all for wealthy millionaires,
But still our Irish lads went down,
With hearts more brave than theirs."

The tragedy lives in some Irish homes even to this day!

My brother Jack was eighteen months younger than I, and we shared most experiences. Jack was a redhead and had the Quinn temper; even at school anyone silly enough to seek an argument with him generally finished it from a reclining position. Jack started work about twelve, with a couple of old bachelors.

Perhaps I should define here a unique practice of employment which has long since become extinct. In May and November each year in the town of Strabane there was what were known as the Hiring Fairs. Here employees and employers met and made contracts for the ensuing six months. The six months following the November Hiring Fair, being winter time, was usually a lean time for employees. Some were willing to work for bed and keep just to tide over the winter. One of the terms was that no matter how bad the conditions were, if the employee left before the term was up, he forfeited all due pay. On the other hand, if the employer sacked an employee then he had to pay for the full term. Conditions of course varied in some instances. It was sad to see little boys of about ten from neighbouring Donegal trying to find work; part of their contract usually stipulated so many hours at school for the hired child, but in most cases this was not honoured.

Though I did go to the Fair sometimes, I never did work under contract; I always worked on weekly hire. I don't think it can be called pride, but I had an aversion to conditions which I felt were an insult to human dignity. It seemed like lumping humans with cattle...or a carry over from the slave market. All this is now I believe under control of a Ministry of Labour which adjust wages and conditions of work. There are of course still many inequalities and "anomalies" and the struggle for the agricultural worker is still a reality.

A Fair Day in Newtown Stewart

Apart from the weekly market day, there was also a monthly Fair. The busy part of the Main Street would be packed with cattle. Cars in those days, the early 1900's, were an exception. My mind retains very vivid memories of those days because even in early years I was a participant, in so far, as I had to help drive the stock the three miles from Uncle Jack's farm into town. Having got into town, the stock would be mustered as far as we were able, to a secure little group where we had to segregate them from the neighbour's stock. It was no easy task, controlling an unruly dozen young stock as well as sometimes cows with calves. Just as we would get them under control along would come the dealers, each armed with an ash plant or cane. They would prod and shove the stock around causing confusion. We would just recover from one invasion when another batch would come along.

The Irish cattle dealer was a unique animal. I don't believe he had a counterpart, unless perhaps in the Bazaars of the East. They would slap hands, slap shoulders, and maybe when the deal got hot, they would shake hands. This was the sign I always dreaded because then Jack and the dealer would retreat to the nearest bar and we would be left to cope as best we could with the animals.

Mention of bars reminds me of the various public houses; from memory there were at least four and Fair Day was heyday for them.

A picture of Newtownstewart's main street on Fair Day. Read Patrick's story of "Fair Day in Newtownstewart" to get the flavor of what it was like, with vendors lining both sides of the street. (c 1920)

===

The hotels and public houses provided stabling, at the back, for their customers' horses and carts, or in the case of the more affluent, a dogcart or a trap. Many times as a boy, I had to yoke up the horse and cart and at a late hour load up with Jack and some drunken cronies who always seemed to be evident after a sale was made, never there to help guard the stock during the day.

When a sale was made, generally after the visit to the bar and with the help of a third person or go-between (I can't recall the Gaelic name for him, but it was very apt), and a bit more spitting on hands and slapping, with an occasional lash at the stock, just to keep us busy, the dealer would put a large chalk mark on the stock purchased.

Some of the dealers represented large export companies but others were just fleas skirting around picking up bargains which would turn up at a neighbouring fair next week and the dealer would hope to sell for a bit of a profit. After the fair sometimes the dealers, as part of the contract, would get us to deliver the animals to the railway station compound half a mile away. If we were lucky we might get a shilling for ourselves, we learnt to know the mean ones. After these deliveries, we would look forward to visiting the side shows and maybe having a drink of lemonade though Jack sometimes forgot we didn't drink ale. Isn't it strange how drinking people will always buy you an ale, but have an aversion to buying a soft drink.

We could look forward to the side shows which were an attraction but sometimes there was another horror in store for us. It was customary for some farmers who hadn't found a buyer to take their stock to a nearby auction yard where if sold they would get the ready cash from the Auctioneer who in turn gave the buyer, as an inducement, thirty days or maybe sixty days to pay, if his credit was good. Now Jack did a bit of dealing and to our horror we would find we had another mob of strange cattle to take home again. On nights like that we had to say good-bye to the side shows.

Jack would graze his new lot for a couple of weeks, then go to a neighbouring Fair and turn over at a bit of a profit...square up the Auctioneer and pocket a few weeks pay. But I can recall one such purchase which turned out to be a disaster. We had got a nice lot of bullocks in fair condition but did not know that they were infected with a bad cattle disease. Uncle Jack lost the lot.

When I looked up the bleak old Main Street in 1978, I tried to recall or rather put myself into my 1913 shoes.

The fair for us was a gala day if we were free, and in later days, it was a day to meet the girlfriend and do the rounds with her. Newtown didn't boast of milk bars as we now know them, but there were a couple of little tearooms where we could entertain, and there was always a quiet nook off the bar for a quiet lemonade. Some of the teeners would drink ale if anybody would serve them. But most of my companions were Pioneers or total abstainers.

Then there were all the confidence men, who would make you believe that you could come to the market barefoot and drive home in a motor car. The only cars I can remember were three battered old trucks, probably Fords, with tray bodies where the hawkers displayed their wares. It was probably something like today's Trash and Treasure or Paddy's Market. The noisy three card men, and the thimble and pea men, were only too willing to relieve youngsters of their spare pennies. That I believe was one of my greatest worries at Fairs and such, lack of cash. I never had enough to go round, odd jobs after work was my only avenue of finance, no allotted pocket money in my day. And odd jobs often turned out to be love jobs, such as, tell your mother if she needs anything from town...which was a great help to me.

Fair Days at Newtown are probably only a memory to my generation. The simple pleasures that satisfied us are no longer acceptable to the present generation. My grandnephews in very early teens were dashing around on motor bikes; I couldn't even attain to a push bike.

* * * * * * *

I was ten years old when the Great World War broke out in 1914. Men and youths I had known went from the district; some never came back. My father volunteered but was rejected which was a relief for Mary Ann. We now entered an era which brought immense upheaval in our lifestyles. Conscription was considered and rejected by the Irish; once it seemed imminent and some of the young men who did not want to go to the war fled to America. Fate played a nasty trick on them. Following the sinking of an American passenger ship the "Luisitania" in 1915, America declared war on the Germans, and many young Irishmen living in America were called up.

Food rationing was stringent. I can still recall the horrible black flour. Housewives in those days all baked their own bread, at least the ones I knew did. There was a baker in our town at one time but he went broke. Back to the flour. It was made out of a mixture of rye, potatoes and a little wheat. Looking back I believe a lot of the rationing and other restrictions was just to make people feel they were making a great sacrifice for the war effort. Rumour was, and I don't doubt it, that many people with money never went short of anything. There was what was known as the Black Market where opportunists made fortunes. War time is always a harvest for opportunists and the higher the positions they hold the bigger the rake off.

People were issued ration cards. I can't recall the exact essence of the ration but it was severe. I was very fond of sugar in my tea and a lot of it. My ration was a few ounces a week so I promptly ceased to use sugar so that mum could have a little extra. Tea leaves were saved and re-stewed. In the main we were not too bad, we had eggs and an odd fowl found its way to the table. Then we got some oats ground for oatmeal and the good old spud.

I can remember Mary Ann dressing a chicken now and then and a carton of eggs for her dear old friends in Glasgow. Many of these donations never reached their destination; there were a lot of hungry people or should I say mean people around. The Irish people would not accept conscription but a deal was made with John Redmond, the leader of the Irish Parliamentary Party in Westminster. If Redmond made a call for a certain number of volunteers to join the British Army, the Government would give home rule to Ireland as soon as the War finished. As we shall see later, things didn't go according to plan and Redmond's reputation suffered as a result.

Neal (my father) got a bit restless about this time; he was immune from call up in England or Scotland, though I, God help me, if I had been of age, would probably have been called up because I was born in Glasgow. It's a legal point of course which did not arise in my case. Neal had news from friends in Glasgow earning up to five pounds a week in a munitions factory, while he was now getting fourteen shillings a week. I don't think Mary Ann took the idea with much favour. Bringing up a family in smelly smoky old Glasgow was not a vision to get rapt about. So we just carried on. Mary Ann raised a brood of turkeys which netted her a nice handful of gold sovereigns. I think some brought five pound each; then a few pigs which had been tended with care brought a few more pounds. All this Mary Ann stowed away against the day when we would get our own little holding, which we eventually did. Eggs were eight or nine shillings a dozen and we had rented a few acres and had some oats and potatoes coming.

CHAPTER FOUR

The War dragged on for four years. In the early years I had a pocket money windfall in the form of blackberries. These grew wild on most farms and in my spare time I headed out with a couple of pails. When I had a good supply I joined my Uncle Jack on his way to the creamery; I was full of excitement and talked about all the money I would get. My Uncle kept damping me off saying they would be not worth much. He was almost as excited as I was when he saw the handful of money I got from the Agent saying he might give up milking cows and take up blackberrying.

I was about eleven and a half years of age in the winter of 1915-16. I had a severe illness from which I was lucky to recover. I developed a virus and double pneumonia. It took me along time to pick up but in the Spring I staggered back to school. I still have scars on my lungs from the effects of that illness. Back at school I felt out of the swim. I had now acquired all that little school had to offer. My worthy old teacher, Master Crampsie, came to our home and presented my father with the proposition that I should study to be a teacher. To do so I would have to attend the Christian Brothers School in Omagh. Only two senior students had gone there from our school in my time.

My ambition was wireless telegraphy which was then in its infancy. A second choice was journalism. Wireless was out. I would have had to go down to Cork to study there. It was all out of the question. How could I, the oldest of six, be supported? Omagh was twelve miles away. We were three miles from the Rail at Newtown Stewart; I didn't even own a pushbike. I would have had to travel by a not very reliable Rail service. It didn't even need thinking about - forget it - just impossible.

Now to today's generation the same distance would be feasible, a fleabite, with fast cars, fast trains, and I guess a different outlook on education. On a recent visit I found a grandniece picked up by bus at her door and taken to Omagh to a consolidated school. The old school of my boyhood was being used as a cattle shelter. I felt like I was witnessing a sacrilege.

Well the decision was made; my loafing days were over. I went to work on the farm where Neal worked. I was appointed second horseman in charge of my own horse and cart, and I was now in a man's domain and there were no apologies. If there was a bag of spuds to lift then I lifted it. If there was a sack of oats to carry then I carried it. Maybe once in a while some kind workmate, noticing my little knees buckling, would lend a hand, but on the whole I did my share. Many nights after swinging a scythe all day cutting heavy meadow grass my back and arms would ache so that I couldn't sleep with the pain and wondered how I'd get up the next morning...don't think I was an exception, many boys like me grew up the same way, at least I had a good home and a good employer. Pity some of the little fellows from poor county Donegal; they often got a hiding and if they ran away or went home they were brought back. Some managed to get off and stow or work their way to England or Scotland where they were probably no better off. No, I'm not whining; if you want to be a farmer you've got to be tough and as Uncle Jack used to say, hard work never killed anyone.

THE CREAMERY AT NEWTOWNSTEWART

CHAPTER FIVE

Easter Week 1916 saw an ill-fated adventure. A body of young men tired of the tactics of the Home Rulers to achieve independence for Ireland decided the time had come to make a dramatic gesture. They set up a movement which became known as the *Sinn Fein (We Ourselves)*. It would take much detail to cover the subject. Members of the Party were from various walks of life; their main ambition was to free their country from English Rule...

> *"a down yon glen on Easter morn, to a city fair rode I,*
> *A mighty throng of marching men,*
> *in squadrons they passed me by,*
> *Right proud and high over Dublin's sky,*
> *they hung out their flag of War,*
> *Weren't it better to die 'neath an Irish sky,*
> *than on Suvla or Seidal Bahr."*

A number of strategic buildings in Dublin were taken over, including the General Post Office. British gunboats shelled the city, causing widespread destruction.. It was a brave but hopeless gesture. The support which had been promised did not materialise and many backed off at the crucial time. Then there was, as always, the informers. After the Easter Uprising had been suppressed most of the leaders were executed by the British, including James Connelly, who was shot while strapped in a chair; because of his wounds he was unable to stand. The brothers Pierce, McBride, whose son has held high rank in the United Nations, only some names remain in memory. De Valera escaped the execution because he was an American citizen.

I can well remember the excitement. Uncle Jack and several of the boys were ready to go, when word came through that it was over. One man was our local doctor. He lived to become a member of the Irish Dail. I had the proud honour, on one occasion, of guarding his motor bike when he walked through the fields to visit a patient. Motors of any sort were rare in our part of the country. I got a reward of two shillings.

"Who fears to speak of Easter week,
Who blushes at the name,
When cowards mock a patriots fate,
Do we hang our heads for shame."

In 1918 the Great War was over. I can say I heard the thunder of guns at the Battle of Jutland and saw my first plane on the ground where it smashed a propeller after making a forced landing. What a difference now; then it was just a series of struts with linen or canvas stretched over. That was my War! Plus, of course, seeing some of the boys home on leave and then seeing the survivors, some minus a leg or arm and some mental wrecks. Glorious War!

The General Post Office in Dublin today

CHAPTER SIX

I was 14. My mother decided that I must get away from being a land slave. I was to learn the grocery trade, sounded good; but it was just one slavery in exchange for another. Two bachelor brothers ran a grocery business in Newtown Stewart. I was going to be initiated into the mysteries of the grocery business. The first couple of weeks I spent weighing and packaging; there was nothing pre-packed in those days. Flour came in eight stone bags, tea came in large chests, that was the bulk tea; expensive tea came in smaller containers; this was used for blending which I will explain...tobacco was in long bars, sugar was in long sacks - all had to be packed and weighed into lots according to demands. It wasn't out of the ordinary for some old lady to come in for two "pennuth" of tea, 1/4 lb. of sugar, maybe two "pennuth" of snuff - fine training for a grocery cadet. Now there's a nice word, none of your apprenticeship rubbish!

Weighing flour, oatmeal or pepper were my pet hates, there was always dust and I suspect I was allergic to it. Tea was a bit of a swindle. There were several grades in nicely embossed bags. The idea was to make the large chests into smaller lots then a few spoonfuls or scoops of choice would be added to the bulk, mixed up and sealed according to grade; price ranged from one shilling and threepence to two shillings and sixpence a pound. Work this all out you metric buffs, me, the old measures will do.

I nearly went bonkers in the first few weeks, seeing nothing but brick walls. I recall one day going to a little enclosure where we kept our horses. There was green grass there, and I was so happy to see green grass I lay down and rolled in it like a dog off the chain. I had been about three weeks at the shop; sometimes I was in the serving counter. There I learnt my first lesson in business. A young girl about my own age came in with a list. I made up the order then she said her mother would pay later in the week. I told the boss, Mick. "Oh," he said, "Did you check the account book?" I hadn't known of the book. We had a check and the family was a bad risk. Then again the girl may have had the money and taken me for an innocent which I was. Should I ask her mother that might mean trouble for the girl. On the other hand, the Boss had told me they only made a convenience anyhow and I wouldn't see her for weeks again. Well I was learning. Next time she came there was extra change so I just stopped what she owed for the earlier lot and told her she could explain to her mother.

Part of the business consisted of going into the country with groceries which were exchanged for farm produce, chiefly eggs and butter. Eggs were a worry when prices went down. People stored them, then when prices went up they would appear with loads of them. I had a fair grounding dealing with eggs and I was able to pick the stale ones, but I was a novice compared to our agent who supervised our packing. He could detect a stale egg a half a mile away.

Some of the runs into the country were one day, others would take three days. We had depots where we laid off our produce and took on more groceries. A truck used to come out and replenish the stores and take back the produce. It was the Boss's ambition to put his own motor truck or van on the road, as it was we had horse power. The country trips were a life saver for me. I got rid of my claustrophobia. The country people were a friendly lot. I was kept busy by the old girls mostly cut off out in the mountains; they rarely got to a town. I was quite willing to get their little bits of ribbon, wool, thread, buttons, or anything that was no weight to carry; I was their white haired boy. Anyhow the Boss said it was good for business, and as I always went to the Draper in town who knew me, he gave me the trade cut and I always charged the proper price, never any more, but at that I still made a bit of pocket money.

Mick was a real happy fellow. I suppose at the time he seemed old to me, but he would probably have been in his late thirties. But that as it may be, he was a bit of a Don Juan; he would have a cuddle with a lady at every cross roads, good for business he would say, as I drove on to the next customer. I often wondered what his brother James would have said if he had known Mick's little aids to business. I don't think I ever saw James smile; he was completely immune to humour.

I lived at the shop, or above the shop. Come Sunday I would go to Mass, then hurry the three miles for a few hours at home. I always went to 9 o'clock Mass. I dreaded going with James; if we happened to get in

**The Roman Catholic Church, St. Eugene's at Glenock (Newtownstewart),
pictured from the graveyard. (2001)**

The story of how Glenock at last got it's cemetery is interesting. Quoting
from the Ulster Herald, Saturday February 14, 1976.
"Three prelates attended the consecration of the new cemetery on
Sunday 23 August 1903, namely, the Bishop of Derry Most Rev. Dr.
O'Doherty, the Castlederg-born Bishop of Goulburn, Australia, Most Rev.
Dr. Gallagher, and the Bishop (later Archbishop of Liverpool, Most Rev.
Dr. Whiteside.

Father O'Doherty had tried for years to obtain land for the cemetery, but
the occupiers of the adjacent land persistently refused to give even a
rood. At last, in frustration he asked one of his parishioners whose land
was a short distance from the church.

This gentleman freely gave all the land required with the result that the church would now have one of the best parochial cemeteries in the Diocese"

The Baptismal Fount, at the Church of St. Eugene, Glenock.

Many of the members of the Kelly family were Baptized here. Neal Kelly (Patrick's father) was most likely the first of the family baptized and the date would have probably been on 26 September 1880. The custom in Ireland, at the time, was to baptize the child on the first Sunday after birth. In this case, Neal was born on 25 September 1880, a Saturday.

A week before this picture was taken (October 2001) someone had placed a pipe bomb on the ledge just outside the window of the Baptistry. The damage caused by the explosion can be seen by the blown out windows and the boarded up frame of the window. There was some external damage to the outside of the structure.

==

just as the Priest fronted the altar, James would decree that we were late and we would have to stay for the 11 o'clock mass. That left me barely two hours at home. Of course it was part of my contract or rule of the job that I was obedient. I can't imagine such obedience from a fifteen year old today though the young people as a whole are probably better than in my youth.

I soon realized that all the young ex-servicemen meeting at the shop of an evening were there for more than card games. *Sinn Fein* was on the move again. This time it was a body of War-tried veterans who thought they had fought for a brave new world only to find they were political footballs or perhaps political derelicts would be a better word. Well, they meant to develop their own political clout and they knew what War was.

After the War an attempt was made to train the disabled to some form of occupation. The scheme was reasonably successful. The able bodied were left to fend for themselves so there was much unemployment; ex-officers were two pence a bunch. No wonder then that the young men were rebelling. An element in Northern Ireland discontent was the schism between the Catholic and Protestant community. Maybe that is an overstatement. Socially for my part I went to dances, sponsored by Protestants and at times played some blatant rebel tunes on my fiddle at their turns.

I believe the schism was kept alive by politicians of both sections, the Protestants wanted to continue alliance with Britain while the Catholics wanted to be pilots of their own destiny. The Protestants with their majority in the North further exacerbated the position by giving preference to their own fellows in most matters, particularly in jobs and housing. For instance, in my case, I would have had a snowball in Hell's chance of getting a job in any Public Service or such, without the backing of an Orangeman. Now my farmer employer was an Orangeman and a fine honest man. I still retain the reference he gave me when I left to emigrate.

I found on my grocery rounds that I was unwittingly delivering seemingly harmless messages to groups in other parts of the country. They would run like this: "Tell old Tom So and So that Jim will be at a certain place at X hours." As most of the people we traveled to were known to me it soon became evident that something was going on. I suspected that my Mick was a *Sinn Fein* sympathizer but for business reasons was neutral. The carriage and passage of arms was a moonlight job and relaying was the method employed. I belonged to the Hibernians who believed in freedom without violence. In analyzing my feelings in later years I believe I was always a Republican, but political events had little bearing on my life.

You know, "Oh Hell!" I hate those words. Every dill on the radio interviews today prefaces and ends his or her phrases with "you know" and always as an interweave in conversation "you know," "you know." Oh damn! I'll try to avoid the evil clichés as much as I can. What I meant to say before I rudely interrupted myself was, I wish to crave an indulgence. I am finding it difficult to keep to that, what did we call it, sequence. Could I just scratch in events as my memory decrees. My capacity for remembering dates has not been much good anyway. Now if I were a writer, I would peruse and research records and verify everything. As it is I can only rely on that little computer at the back of my cranium or wherever it is situated. And who am I to complain if after 70 years of usage it may be getting a bit hazy or muzzy. All I can say is Lord thank you for the faculties I am allowed to retain. Another horrible thought - can you be sure what I write will be true? Well, you can't really be, but an Irishman's bond is his word.

CHAPTER SEVEN

The Great War started 1914, 14th August. It may have been that year or the year prior that Mary, the youngest of our family was born. She was a healthy baby, but Mary Ann developed septicemia. She was rushed off to Omagh hospital where she had a long struggle to survive. In later years I fully appreciated how dad must have felt. I kept the home while Aunt Kate, a little work worn spinster coped with the new baby.

I'd better explain here the usual practice among the poorer people anyhow; the babies were born at home, in most cases without a doctor and with questionable hygiene. An elderly woman neighbour with home acquired skill acted as midwife, little difference from the Australian bush in the 1800's. If there were complications a doctor would be called. Whether he got there on time was another matter. Sometimes weeks before the birth these kind women would come and assist the expectant mother. Well, that's what good neighbours are meant to do.

It was probably 1920 (again no records) as an aftermath to the holocaust of War a curious deadly illness scourged the land; it was called the Black Flu. Many people died; in most cases it was the strong and healthy who succumbed. It was sudden in its impact too. I nursed Jack and Kate Quinn doing all the farm work too. Luckily it was off season and the cows were dry so there was not much milking but the animals have to be fed. I coped. When Jack and Kate were on their feet again, my own family folded up en masse. I was the lucky one; again I nursed, cooked, and was a general dogs body; eventually all recovered. Mary Ann seemed to have a carry over from her previous ordeal; in fact, she was never the same virile person that she had been.

It was Christmas Eve; I was going to see a young friend reported to be dying. I hadn't gone far when I felt like I had been shot, everything started to spin; so this was what the Flu was like. I called out, and luckily my girlfriend heard me and she managed to drag me or half carry me home. Maybe I will tell you of that dear girl later. It was many long cold winter weeks before I recovered the evil Flu and then a second bout of pneumonia. God must have had plans for my future. I had survived the Black Flu from which many had died. It was, I believe, a world-wide epidemic.

I had now left the shop and was back at the farm at my old job again. I recall one little incident from the shop particularly well. The people next door, whose yard was one with the shop, had a little dog. The shop had a big attraction for him. He had a nasty habit of mistaking bags of flour and sugar for posts and missed no opportunity to irrigate them. I had just caught him in the act, and as a deterrent and punishment I took him out by the scruff and held his head under the water tap. Then a Fury landed on my shoulders in the shape of a small girl. I was roundly abused by the little virago. She was older than her size suggested. Later we became close friends and we corresponded for years; she has long since gone to God.

As I noted before, my little mother, Mary Ann, didn't seem her old self; her eyesight was not good through too much straining. I often recall her crouched over the old Singer sewing machine trying to thread the needle. Now she suffered from arthritis which further hindered her. Many times I would wake up in the night to hear the machine whirring away on some rush job. Like the other dear woman in my life, my partner of fifty years, she was always sewing something for someone, maybe a baby outfit or a wedding frock, mostly all love jobs. As time went by, the arthritis got worse. I was the mechanical expert when the Singer got the tantrums which it usually chose to do when there was a rush job. Funny thing about my dad; give him a chisel and saw and he could make anything; he could sew the soles on a pair of shoes and there was plenty of those to do, but the sight of a screw driver used to make him wince.

Grandma Rosy had died, and her home was occupied by Aunt Margaret, who had come over from America, to care for her. Margaret had married and wanted to go back to the States, so the old home was for sale. Dad thought it fitting that we buy it. So Mary Ann's little nest egg was disbursed and we had our own home. There was not a large amount of land but we could always rent some more. My sister Mary$_2$ and her husband live there. I slept there in 1978 after an absence of 53 years. It is a very ancient little home; incidentally the old cottages in Gallon have been nearly all replaced by new homes and the face of the land is changing.

$_2$ Ed. note - Mary has since died, in 1981.

The first remodel of the Kelly farm home. There are no pictures of the house without the bay that was added. The current owners, Tess and William John Patton are shown in the doorway.

After my return to the farm work, tragedy struck us. I was working in a quarry in company with my father's brother, Uncle Bill. Bill was a big gentle giant and we got on well together. He had two daughters, just a quiet hard working man. On this particular day, it was about noon, and we were just knocking off for the mid-day meal. My little brother Dan, and Mary had just come along to speak to us. Bill looked back, a large rock was projecting from the quarry wall. Bill said, "That looks bad, it could easily crash on the children like these if they went under." So he grabbed a crowbar and jabbed at the rock. Without any warning several tonnes of earth came down over him. I rushed in, and the second fall from the nearer top passed over me. I said to the children, "Run for help!" I don't know how I managed to roll the large rocks and earth off him; he died in my

In Loving Memory Of
JEANNIE KELLY
DIED 29TH APRIL 1978
HER PARENTS   WILLIAM KELLY
DIED 23RD JULY 1919
KATHLEEN ANN KELLY
DIED 19TH AUGUST 1929
R I P

Gravestone of members of the Kelly family. William, (Uncle Willie) was one of Patrick's favorite uncles. Uncle Willie died in Patrick's arms after a huge boulder and earth fell upon him in a nearby quarry in Gallon Sessiagh.

arms. For a long time afterwards, I used to leave the bed screaming as the walls would seem to be falling in on me. That scene is etched on my mind. Just a brief account here can give no idea what sudden death can do to a boy's mind. One of Bill's daughters, my cousin, has corresponded with me down the long years. She knew I was visiting Ireland; we looked forward to meeting. She died three weeks before my visit.

I believe I must have had a very diligent guardian angel. Some years after my escape in the earth fall that caused Uncle Bill's death, I was engaged in mining some sand from [a] pit a few miles from the home farm, situated in a lonely spot, and I was working alone. The sandpit carried a heavy overburden of soil. A deep pit had been dug and the sand was scooped out from the cave-like opening and shoveled up to the ground above. The pit was about seven feet deep, and I had gouged some steps out of the side as a means of exit.

It was evening and almost knock-off time. I did not intend going back to the farm that evening. I would have had to backtrack a few miles, as I intended going to a card party. Suddenly I noticed a trickle of sand from the pit top, and some movement. I dropped tools and dived for the steps. When the cave-in started, it caught my legs and there was a mighty rush of air as the pit filled up.

Had I been buried there, no one would have known until a check next day. I was not expected at the farm and my family would probably have been asleep when I got home from the card party...happy escape, and the end result was an order for two men always to work together in such circumstances. I've had some close calls but those two incidents were very close.

* * * * * * *

It is not pleasant to dwell on too much sorrow yet life is like that and we just have to play the cards that are dealt; I know there is a sort of a movement today towards opting out and I have never felt like that. I suppose you guess by now that I write this under pressure. You see I made a contract (I hate that word) with my rich Uncle Barney in America to write a memoir to comprise of X number of pages. There is a bonus for every page over a thousand. I can't do it. Here I am still only on page 31.[3] Uncle is a pretty mean old skunk; I suppose that comes of making a lot of money or was it maybe the other way round? (Uncle Barney is a family myth).

[3] Ed note: "page 31" refers to the author's original handwritten manuscript.

CHAPTER EIGHT

I don't think I gave much insight into my schooldays. I was almost seven when I got to school. I could already read and write, tutored by my mother who had been a trainee teacher before being forced to give up by the death of her mother. I believe in all the 60 pupils I could always hold my own and even though I lost time through illness and work pressure, I always passed my exams. History? Well I learnt that in 1014 Brian Boru slew twenty Danes before breakfast! Then there was that champion runner, James the second Stuart. He was in such a hurry to get off to France where he had a tryst with the wife of one of the Louis's. He was in such a hell of a hurry he left his pyjamas behind in the castle at Newtown Stewart. That castle, by the way, was built by another Stewart, no relation to James, who burnt the castle, and part of the town, pyjamas and all, before leaving.

Then I learnt about Oliver Cromwell and the great Commonwealth of England. The Irish had no time for Ollie who told some of my ancestors to get to Hell or Connaught. They said, "Ollie, there would be no room for you and us in Hell so we'll go to Connaught." Ollie had a cousin or something of a later vintage; his name was Winston Churchill. There was no nonsense about Winnie. There was a race-horse named after Winnie in Australia. Most Australian race-goers will remember Windbag. I don't think there are any statues to Winnie anywhere in Ireland.

My knowledge of history was really good. I remember Horrie Nelson, he lost an arm by dangling it over the side of a life boat in icy water, frost bite; some say he was asleep but the London Times said he was drunk. He was the boy who started the saying, a lady in every Port. Have you had enough? Well there was the fellow with the big boots, Wellington; he started a duck farm or something over in Flanders. You may remember the tripe they used to tell us about Bob Bruce (the Scotch lap it up). He was supposed to be bitten on the backside by a spider while sleeping in the hayshed. I think it may have been a rat, whatever it was, the poison was so potent he got going and knocked the bedamnits out of the English at Bannockbyrn. (Check that). Oh then, in a later War, there was Kitchener who coined the saying, "Up guards and at 'em." On second thoughts I think that may have been Mae West at the Battle of Broadway. Or did she say, "Pull up your socks Richard, you are in deep water." Yes, I think I could still do H.S.C. in History.

Well, General Knowledge. I was a bit slow there, and I get my future es mixed up with the past. But it is common knowledge that America and Russia control two thirds of the world, Japan controlled all Northern Australia, and a coloured named Young was President of America!! I think it was Bill Shakespeare who said, "a little nonsense now and then is relished by the best of men." Now there's a thought. Why wasn't Bill ever knighted or something. Yes, I know he is treated as a Saint in the English midlands and they sell little medallions and all sorts of memoir. But he is dead now.

It's a strange thing, just another thought, why do we always wait until a man is gone to eulogize him. It doesn't matter if he wasn't a very wholesome sort of person in life. We always find a little build up once he's gone. There are of course exceptions, like tax collectors or politicians. Though mind you some of them can be almost human at times.

CHAPTER NINE

"They came from a land beyond the sea,
Now O'er the western Main.
Set sail in their good ships gallantly,
From the sunny land of Spain."

It's not so easy as that Ireland has been a melting pot of many peoples. In later history the races have merged and royal blood has mixed with the common and people formed into clans or family tribes. Invasions were often, and in most cases, the original inhabitants were forced further back into the rocky and even bleak westlands. It's true too there is Spanish blood in the South as late as 1600. A large army of Spanish came to assist the Irish in their struggle.

I believe my ancestors were the very early originals, the small dark men, our clan, the *O'Ceallaigh,* lived in the northern part of Connaught, a tract of land called HY, which means Kelly's land. I can't be absolutely sure about all this, the Kelly's are now legion. I did do some genealogical research years ago but it's very involved and through the years much blood mixtures have occurred with marriage. My mother's family, the O'Quinns, were also of the same genre. There are the main clan O'Quinn in Co. Clare, ours were the Ulster branch.

To get some glimmer of understanding of what is known as the Irish question from the past up until the present, one will have to remember the invasions and plantations by force on the Irish people. The two issues which probably had the greatest impact were the Norman invasion of the South under Strongbow, and the Elizabethan Plantation of Ulster.

The southern foray was in a way, beneficial to Ireland, because the Normans, mostly Catholic, fitted into the Irish environment, intermarried with the native Irish, and eventually joined them in their rejection of England. When the name Fitzgerald, Fitzpatrick, or other such names are mentioned, the remark will be, "No need to ask where he comes from." Well, you'll see history will tell you he is a Norman descendant. Then there are the Delacys, Delaneys or Degaris, again Norman, then the anglicized version of such - Fitzmaurice (Morris), Fitzalan (Allen) - all good Irishmen. Then let's not forget all those other good Irish patriots who gave their life for Ireland and they were the Protestant descendants of Englishmen from the Pale.

The Plantation of Ulster was something different. This Plantation which, in my opinion, was the cause of most of the dissension in the North today, was the planned settlement of thousands of Scottish Presbyterians and others following the religion of King Henry VIII. These people abhorred the native Irish and their Catholic Religion. The fact that they did not intermarry was probably the fault of both sides. Rome forbade a Catholic to marry a Protestant and vice versa. And so the schism remained and widened. The burning cause of hatred was the confiscation of lands which were bestowed on the English Lords and high ranking officers. Some of the originals were allowed to farm their own land after paying a heavy yearly toll to the newly created landlord. In most cases the newcomers were put in possession of all the choice farmland while the original owners were hunted into the hungry glens and mountains. Undoubtedly the present generation whether Protestant or Catholic are Irishmen and Irishwomen. They were born and reared in Ireland and think it unfair that they should be blamed for the sins of their forefathers, but there is the thorn. Five hundred years ago is just as vivid to the average Irishman as yesterday.

On the credit side of the invaders, they did much to improve the country. Whole new towns were built and large new industries were fostered. Many men from the other isles invested in transport and other ploys which, while recognizing the self interest, also went some way to relieving poverty. Why then did the Irish Catholic resent and still resent his Protestant neighbour? The answer is twofold. Apart from being a very meek race, the Irish are also very proud, and most men with a scrap of virility want to be masters of their own destiny. Secondly, as I have already stated, the Catholic was treated almost as a second rate citizen in so far as employment in Public Service or other remunerative jobs were concerned. It is true that wealthy Catholics have obtained positions of note in the land, but on a pro rata basis they fell short. As for the children of the poor, the dice was and is still slightly against them.

Another body of the invaders, or should I say among the invaders, were the Huguenots (refugees from Catholic France); who were Protestant.

They brought with them many crafts and skills and were of benefit to the land.

"Ye Geraldines, ye Geraldines,
'Tis full a thousand years,
Since mid the Tuscan Vineyards bright,
Flashed your battle spears.
Across the sands of Hastings,
You spurred hard by William's side,
And those old gray sands of Palestine
With Moslem blood you dyed."

CHAPTER TEN

It was 1920. The Black and Tans were ravaging the land. They were a motley force recruited from the riffraff in England to combat the Irish Republican Army and to counter the rising surge of Nationalism among the Irish. The Tans were no credit to England and their atrocities were well recorded. Feeling throughout America and the ordinary decent people of England rose to a frenzy of anger when some of the dark deeds of the Tans were known. Cork, a large city in the South, was gutted. Women and children were mistreated. Now for heaven's sake, don't visit onus for these crimes on the ordinary English citizen. They were in some cases in need of the freedom as much as the Irish.

It was always the strategy of the English politicians and overlords to divide and conquer; in this case they threw the Northern Protestants against the people of the South. The minority Protestants in the South were quite happy to have self-government and all seemed to live in harmony in the new Irish Free State. We, in the North, were under martial law, [and] then a curfew was proclaimed. That meant that anyone abroad after 10pm without a permit, risked being shot. A special part-time force was recruited from young Protestants willing to serve. Actually the force, known as the "B Special Constabulary" could have contained either religion and a few Catholics did join in. After a few incidents, where a couple of young

Catholics were shot, it soon became evident that Catholics were not wanted in the "B Specials".

If we wanted to hold a dance, a permit had to be obtained and no one could go further than twenty feet from the vicinity of the dance hall. The Specials were usually in attendance to carry out the regulations. If the patrol was comprised of local boys we had no trouble; one of their number would look after the rifles while the other would join in the fun. But if we were unlucky to get a patrol from town, then there could be trouble. Of course the Tans or the Military were different; they were savages!

I had made the acquaintance of a young Protestant girl and with the exuberance of youth we thought we were meant for each other. Her father, a wealthy farmer probably had other thoughts which he did not voice. In company with my cousin Willie, who had good reason for going too, we would go to this district on a Sunday afternoon; it was a predominantly Protestant district. One particular Sunday, we had been with the girls to a Crossroads dance and arrived back at their home by dusk, and chasing curfew time. We were told that a Specials Patrol were on to us and meant to take us. The Patrol, we were told, was comprised of town men who had no time for us so we had better watch out. We had one advantage; we knew every inch of the country, which the town men didn't. It was almost dark when we spotted them so we took to the ditches. My hair started to rise when I heard the whistle of the first bullet. It is a queer feeling to be treated as a rabbit. You know, I never held with violence or capital punishment but if I had had a rifle that night I would have killed or shot to kill. So now I know how old Ned felt.

CHAPTER ELEVEN

The story of Ireland is apt to get a bit boring, yet I have a feeling if we don't know where we came from then we never know who we are. So I believe people from all countries should at least know the bones of their history and that applies especially to Australians.

In 1922 all Hell broke loose in Ireland. A Treaty had been signed by delegates representing the I.R.A. under coercion from Lloyd George, the then English Prime Minister. The Treaty would give Ireland self-government. Northern Ireland or the Protestant majority rejected the Treaty and started an all out blitz on all people suspected of being I.R.A. supporters. That meant a person could be picked up, held for X number of days, released and picked up again the same day, and to Hell with the Magna Charta.

I got into a bit of a bother at home, but it could have been worse. Some of the boys had alerted us that a search was going on in all the houses, and if anything of a suspicious nature was found, off you went to the Argenta, a prison ship anchored in Belfast Lough. I showed the boys an old Army (British) training manual that I had picked up in the second-hand bookshop. "Oh," they said, "You would be gone a million if they found that." Then I had some diagrams of signaling equipment and how to make a wet battery, another illegal possession. I was interested in wireless telegraphy and signaling. Anyhow, the boys took it all to a safe place.

After the Treaty, Civil War broke out in the South, brother against brother; it was horrible. Men who had fought as comrades were now fighting each other. And some were even condemned to death. I will go no further on this as the knowledge can be had from any public library, where varied accounts will be found. I will, however, make a private assertion that the men who made the Irish Republic a reality were not the men who sat in the Dail. The men who did the fighting were forced to get out of the country, while the privileged class who sat on their fat bottoms when the struggle was on, took over.

Indeed it was the fault of the large property and business men that the half-baked Treaty was forced on Collins and his men. The result of refusal meant a full onslaught on the country, and of course property would have been destroyed. But men had already given their lives. In fact, there is no real representation of the ordinary working man in Eire up to date. So, in my opinion, they are no better off than under England.

Maybe here I should deplore the fact that people masquerading as the I.R.A. in Ireland today are in my opinion anarchists, foreign terrorists and communists and no good will come to Ireland through their efforts. It is strange that the English working man who has experienced the same hardships as his Irish neighbor continues to reject communism.

CHAPTER TWELVE

On the home front, things were miserable. We had a wet summer, in fact, we had two whole wet years and when it rains in the North, it rains! The clouds roll in from the Atlantic, over the Mountains of Donegal. I can honestly say that for two years we rarely ever saw the sun. Once in a while a certain pale circle would appear and you knew that behind all the grey banks of cloud a feeble sun was hopelessly enshrouded. We relied for heating on turf fires; there was no weather for turf drying……..

Turf and Turf Cutting

To sit beside the turf fire in the cabin,
And watch the barefoot gossins at their play.

The smell of the turf fire burning is a nostalgic memory to many an Irish migrant. In all the country areas, the main heating power was turf or dried peat. The production of turf in my day was vastly different from what it is today, especially, in Eire where it is mass handled by machinery which cuts, dries and presses.

Peat is the end result of thousands of years of decayed vegetation. It differs in location, one variety is in marshy bogs, the best and most favoured is found on the mountain plateaus. The process in my day was to select the site and a swathe about six feet wide would be opened; the top layer would be removed and discarded, then up to four floors or layers would be dug out. The implement for cutting was a spade with arranged grips on the handle, and a sharp winged blade. The turf about fourteen inches long were handled in pairs by a labourer known as the filler, a job at which I served my time, a back-breaking job. The filler heaved the heavy turf on to a shovel or barrow which was deposited in neat rows by the bank man. I felt very proud when I graduated to be a cutter which was considered a skilled job and sometimes rated the princely sum of four shillings a day.

Four or five layers were taken out in this fashion. The cut out ground would eventually be five or six feet lower, and in marshy areas turned into a swamp. When the turf acquired some skin through sun drying, they were turned over. If wet weather intervened a furry surface would slow the drying and on windy days the dust was an irritation. The whole process was a tedious backbreaking toil. On calm days the bogs were invaded by hordes of midges; these little pests were worse than mosquitoes and raised a large itch rash.

Once the cutting was done the further harvesting was carried out by women folks and children, so there was never any lack of work for small hands. Many an hour Mary Ann with myself as assistant would spend turning and ricking so that we would have warm fires for winter. All the while Jack would be keeping guard over the little ones to see that they didn't vanish into a bog hole, and make sure the baby in its basket was not tormented by the midges. Oh, there was always a baby!

Speaking of the bog holes, I have heard a derogatory term used here when speaking of the Irish: "Oh, he was just a drag up from the bogs of Ireland," something I suppose like the hillbillies of America. Well, Ireland is not all bogs, and whatever, bogs or riverflats, many countries owe a huge debt to that little green blob in the Atlantic. The History of Australia is dotted with the names of Irishmen who have enriched the culture of their new home.

Retrogressing back to the turf, imagine my surprise on my visit to the old house to find my sister burning coal. Turf, unlike coal, burns clean and has a unique pleasant odour. A couple of wet seasons had spoilt the turf harvest, hence the coal fires. The first year we cut down every available tree; green wood doesn't burn very well. How mum coped with the cooking I don't know. Perhaps I should issue a plea here to all young people in your youthful careless and sometimes arrogant behaviour, please give a little more time to your mother. I loved my mother, but in many remorseful heart searchings, I believe that I should have realized that she was slowly fading, and we youngsters were wrapped up in our social life and our own affairs.

As the wet continued I got more and more fed up with things. We would come home soaking wet and next morning our boots and work clothes would still be damp and eventually mouldy, no electric heaters and dryers in those days. We still had kerosene lights, the town was gaslight. The harvest mostly rotted in the ground as did the potatoes. I recall my final rebellion. I was cutting oats with a scythe; it was so flattened with storms that the reaper mower could not handle it. I had to pick it up and lay it out in the unbound sheaves. The water oozed from it and I was cold and sodden. I seized the scythe and hurled it into the crop and walked home. I got a pen and wrote an urgent plea to Aunt Nell in America to see if she would sponsor me into the States. No luck. Nell had nominated two other cousins in the previous year. Wait for a year or so she said. True, she wrote to me twelve months after I came to Australia telling me she had found a job for me. Probably I was still a bit sulky so I said I was happy in Australia.

It was around this time I copped a dose of pleurisy which finished up with pneumonia and nearly finished me. The doctor warned me that I could not afford to get it again. The winter was over, as if one could notice the difference, but it had been severe. Advertisements were appearing in the paper blaaing about the great prospects of a new life in Canada. Oh well, I thought, any port in a storm. It cost very little to get there, but as we found out later, a hell of a lot to get out. My cousin, Bill Dolan, was also interested, one of our neighbours had already gone there so we wrote and asked him what it was like. After a lapse of time, we got a letter saying it was all right and he had jobs for us. Now to contact the Canadian Immigration people. Soon everything was falling into place. We would say good-bye to Ireland.

A large batch of boys and some girls were off to America. We had a round of send-off parties; we kept our own travel arrangements secret. I can remember going down to football practice only to realize that half our team had gone. I can still recall that awful feeling of loneliness that came over me. Some of the boys gone were from an earlier age but others were schoolmates. I had always suffered a bit from loneliness but I went and sought solace in the company of my girl mate whom I have already mentioned. She said, "let's go to Canada." I wondered then if someone had been talking. I felt guilty because I had not told her of our plans that Bill and I had for Canada.

CHAPTER THIRTEEN

Mary Ann was ill and we knew it had to be serious for her to admit it. It was autumn and Canada in the fall was not a good picture. I couldn't leave while Mary Ann was ill; she asked me to stay until she was well again, which I promised. So the Canada voyage was canceled. I carried on at the farm, another miserable winter which I dreaded with my limping lungs.

A close friend and school mate had two brothers who had returned from a long period in Australia. They had married and settled down to farming, having saved enough money in Australia to buy their farms. I used to meet them and have long talks about Australia and they fired me with all the talks of the beautiful sunshine and all the lovely Queensland beaches, and all the lovely girls.

> *"Farewell and adieu to you Brisbane ladies,*
> *Farewell and adieu to the girls at Tawong,*
> *We have sold all our cattle and cannot now linger,*
> *But we hope we will see you again before long."*

But Charlie and Bill never saw Australia again. In correspondence they told me they were homesick for Australia but their wives said no.

It was a cold March night. I was sitting up with Mary Ann; she had gradually faded. We had tried hard to persuade her to go to the hospital but some worry from her earlier time in the hospital had made her scared of going, so there was nothing we could do, just rely on the doctor. In these days of improved care, there would have been some avenue of hope. In

The grave of Patrick's father, Neal and his mother Mary Ann Quinn Kelly. Her death in 1924 delayed Patrick's departure from Ireland. It certainly changed his life forever. Prior to Mary Ann's death, Patrick had planned to go to Canada. Instead he traveled to Australia where his destiny led him to the love of his life, Dulcie (Doreen) Redenbach.

==

some way she had lost the will to go on. Some time on that night while I kept vigil she left us and went to God. She was only in her mid-forties. Down the years as I have matured I have worried and tortured myself thinking about her, wondering why it had to be like that, and was there something we had left undone. It could not be; there were all the senior people and the doctor who did all they could. Mary Ann had seemed tired without the will to carry on. She had fulfilled God's plan for her.

Even had the opportunity been there, I could not leave Dad at this time. I just had to settle down for a while. Sister Cassie, then in her teens, took over the reins of the household. My loneliness was now increased worse than ever, but life had to go on. Perhaps I could now introduce the girl mate I have mentioned; her name was Kathleen shortened to Katie. She was three years my senior but we met at school and after various partings and makings up we drifted together. For my part she was like an older sister. We went to dances, we went to excursions; there was one drawback, Katie's people were farmers and she was always flush with pocket money which I could not afford to match. Her home was only 200 yards from ours so it was not possible to miss each other. I don't think I ever entertained any idea of marriage but I think at times Katie may have thought it possible. To me she was a good friend and companion and like myself she was a member of our Temperance Society. It was not feasible for me to mix and travel with the boys as most of them drank and on a day out could become perfect nuisances, and I abhor alcohol. I don't think I loved her in the accepted meaning of the word but she was a dear, dear person to me and filled a large part of my boyhood. She walked with me to the Rail when I left home. She taught me this song from which I now quote a meaningful part which was a promise:

"But if you come when all the flowers are dying,
And I be dead as dead I well may be,
You will come and find the place where I am lying,
And say an Ave there for me."

In 1978 I visited Ireland. I found Katie had gone to God, but no one could tell me where she rested. The promise was unfulfilled.

Nocturne

(written for Katie)

The bloom is on the heather, and summer is in the air,
The exile is returning, but you will not be there.
The paths we trod are still the same, and time has not erased
The memory of secrets shared, which will never be replaced.
The schoolhouse is lone and desolate, where we spent our childhood days,
'Ere the waft of Fate decided, that we go our separate ways.
But the bloom of friendship flourished, though we were far apart,
And the hope that we would meet again, was anchored in our heart.
And there upon the river bridge, our initials etched in stone,
The river paths we wandered, I travel now alone.
Memory is a precious gift that makes our world worthwhile,
What pleasure when we can recall a handshake or a smile.
The thoughts of youth are vivant, and tomorrow is always there,
The world is ours to conquer and our victories we must share.
But down the corridors of time the years have swiftly went,
The world is still unconquered and our youthful vigours spent.

'Farewell, dear friend, farewell, I bid you fond good-bye,
But I will treasure you in memory, until the day I die.
And when my maker calls me, this I know he will say,
Your friend is out there waiting, and everything's O.K.'

CHAPTER FOURTEEN

After the loss of my mother, and the departure for America of many good friends, the bottom seemed to have fallen out of my world. Again in the company of my cousin Bill, it was decided that we try for Australia. I was entrusted with all the paperwork and getting of information. I contacted an agent in London, who in turn put me in contact with a local agent in Omagh. This time there was no secrecy of our intentions and in no time there was a long list of intending migrants. I continued with the plans aided by my friends who had lived in Australia. They made me aware of conditions and the pitfalls to be avoided.

By the time we had to go for a final interview and a medical scan, our group had dwindled to two. My cousin didn't satisfy the medical exam, and others just lost the spirit of adventure. With myself was Dan, an older neighbour, who had just finished a term in the Eire Army. Cousin Bill was later sponsored by his brother in America. My brother Jack was keen on coming, but my dad reckoned it was better I do a bit of scouting first.

> *"And I'm praying to God on high,*
> *And I'm praying Him night and day,*
> *For a little house, a house of my own,*
> *Out of the wind and the rain's way."*
> *~P. Colum~*

Why do I seek to foster that link with Ireland, when the most it could give me was hard work and misery? What is the indefinable something, which makes magic, the little green lump of soil in the Atlantic, called Ireland? For me I suppose it is the memory that the dust of my ancestors is merged with Irish soil and there are still lots of my kin living there.

> *"How sleep the brave who sink to rest,*
> *By all their countries wishes blest,*
> *When Spring with dewy finger cold*
> *Returns to deck their hallowed mould."*
> *~W. Collins~*

One often wonders too when the word Ireland is mentioned even in remote parts of the globe, people will start scrounging in their genealogical cupboards hoping to find some thread of ancestry which will link them to Ireland. (I think I mentioned previously the innate modesty of the Irish). It is common knowledge in Australian History that when Captain Jim Cook first came to Botany Bay, he was met there by Irishman Bennalong, with a bottle of poteen in one hand and a shillelagh in the other. And those other Irish in Hawaii regarded Cook with such esteem that they !!!! I think we will leave this one till after lunch!

You are again questioning the veracity of my historical statements. Well, I can assure you since your last complaint I have done a patient research having had full access to the Historical Library at Tangmalangmaloo where all the Nation's historical records are sealed away.

It can be conceded however that historians, like politicians, get a bit cross-eyed at times. One chappie had the cheek to say that Ned Kelly died from a broken neck. You may remember the story of Ned. I heard a whisper that he is being investigated with a view to canonization. About the history. Just to allay any doubts you may have, I will at all times survey those historical times with both eyes open, and I'm not cross-eyed (I hope). Stemming from this, there is at the back of my mind an ambition to write a complete history of Australia, starting with Billy Hughes and Roy Rene. This will require a lot of research. Then there is another treatise which could be quite interesting. Why do politicians always have shiny seats to their pants? I think there are some wide areas for research there.

Verse...A breeze mid blossoms straying,
Where hope clung feeding like a bee,
Both were mine, life went maying,
With Nature, Hope and Poesy.
Dew drops are gems of morning,
But the tears of mournful Eve.
Where no Hope is; life's a warning
That only serves to make us grieve
When we are old.

~S.T. Coleridge~

CHAPTER FIFTEEN

I was busy preparing for the departure. It was the winter after mam's death. Dad was battling on though much had changed; he was always a cheery man and a great singer, always in demand at local concerts. I regret that circumstances prevented me from ever meeting him again, though he lived on to his mid-eighties. He was a kind, peaceful man, though I saw him intervene once when two thugs had attacked Uncle Jack. He lifted both bodily and threw them over a fence.

I was short of money so I went to see Uncle Jack where I borrowed 40 or 50 pounds. On a cold frosty morning at the end of January, Uncle Jack conveyed us into Newtown Stewart where I made a round of many friends. I had already said good-bye to all the district neighbours. It was a custom (and a very good one) to always give the departing traveler a silver coin, florin or crown; my pockets were bulging with silver.

Dad noticed in town that one of my suitcases looked like rupturing so he hied off to the saddler and came back with a strap to bind it. I still retain that strap as a memory and it served me for years as a belt. A link with my dear Father. At last we boarded the train for Belfast and the cross channel boat. It was dark when we arrived in Belfast and it was snowing.

When I came to Belfast in 1978 it was raining, and a British rifleman stood at every corner!

**Neal Kelly and daughter Mary (Patrick's father and sister)
(c. 1930)**

"Uncharted is our course, our hearts untried,
And we may weary 'ere we take the tide,
Or make fair haven from the moaning sea."
~J. Stephens~

The Kelly Home in Gallon upper as it looks today, [2001], after a major remodel by the present owners, Tess and Willie John Patton. Tess is Patrick's niece.

BOOK TWO
The Emigration - Immigration Years

BOOK TWO

Is there for honest poverty wha' hangs,
his head and a that
The coward slave we pass him by
We daur be puir for a that.
~Burns~

Lord, Thou has said, "When you
have toiled and tilled
When you have borne the heat
and wisely sown
And every corner of the vineyard
filled
With goodly growth, the land shall
be your own.
Then shall your sons and your sons'
sons rejoice!"
~Dennis~

The moving finger writes, and having writ,
Moves on; nor all thy piety not wit
Shall lure it back to cancel half a line,
Nor all thy tears wash out a word of it.
~D. Khayyam~

CHAPTER ONE

My life after Ireland will start at twenty, and I am aboard a cross channel boat bound for London on the first leg of a journey to Australia, where according to the loads of literature I had from the migration people and their agents, life would be happy and carefree in a great land warmed by beautiful sunshine. And an added lure was the promise of a large section of land just waiting there to be tilled, and as the blurb stated, it's a poor farmer who can't make prosperity with 640 acres of free, fertile soil! I had taken all this with the proverbial grain of salt. I had been wised-up by a couple of neighbours who spent some years during the 1900's in the country.

When they found out I had selected the State of Victoria as my destination, they expressed some doubts about my wisdom. One of them said he wouldn't let his little dog die in scabby Victoria. They had spent their years in N.S.W. and Queensland where the Victorians allegedly had a reputation as job snatchers and strike breakers.

But as I have stated, here I was on the cross channel bound for London; memory has not registered my first port - maybe Holyhead or Birkenhead. At that time I didn't care; I was violently seasick. I was accompanied by another chap, Dan, from my home district. Unable to put up with the smoke and smell of vomit from other passengers, I wandered up on deck. It was a howling gale and snowing very hard. I can recall a deckhand pushing me, not too gently, down the companionway (which is what I think is the nautical term for stairway). And I not caring if I had been allowed to go overboard, going head first down the stairway, when a strong arm went round me. Jack was a boy from my home county and our friendship lasted for many years, till the cares of family let us drift our separate ways.

January is not the best month to see London. We had three or four days to spend there before we joined the ship at Tilbury for Australia, the hotel where we were booked in was packed with intending migrants like ourselves, many from Ireland and the many Scottish Isles; all had decided that prospects in the homeland were limited.

My traveling mate, a neighbour from home, had knocked around, and being near ten years my senior, took more easily to the changing scenes and strange companions. After the quiet rural scenes of my home, London at first was a big headache, but I gradually got used to the noise. Visibility was limited by constant fog. But the London Bobbies were wonderful. The nickname "Bobbies" I understand originated from the founder, or one of the people responsible for the formation of the London police, one Sir Robert Peel, hence the name "Bobbie's men," or sometimes caustically referred to as "Peelers". Be that as it may, our contact with the force, which meant every street corner, was heaven sent, because we were continually lost. But with a Bobby's aid, we always arrived back safe out our hotel.

One little incident sticks in my mind, and tends to strengthen warnings to youth never to get involved with strangers. My mate, Dan, myself and Jack, were inspecting a shop window displaying Australian souvenirs when we were joined by a large prosperous looking gentleman, beaming with goodwill. I noticed he was sporting a large double watch chain across his ample chest. On the chain dangled a gold cross and two silver kangaroos; this suggested he might have had some connection with Australia.

Jack, the gregarious fellow at all times, was soon giving him all the details of our journey. He told us he was a Mr. O'Brien on a visit from N.S.W. Undoubtedly of Irish origin. By a strange coincidence he was going home on the Moreton Bay, which was the ship we were to travel on. At Mr. O'Brien's suggestion, it was decided we get a bus down to Australia House. He offered to pay our fares. I paid my own, I didn't quite take to Mr. O'Brien. We got off a bus outside a bank, where Mr. O'Brien proceeded to relate to Jack that it would be to his advantage to change his English money to Australian currency. He had a friend in the bank who would help give a profitable exchange. I saw daylight and said to Jack that I was perfectly capable of exchanging my own money. Dan said he agreed with me. What transpired between Jack and Mr. O'Brien I never knew, maybe he parted with some notes. Mr. O'Brien said to wait outside and he disappeared inside the bank. We waited for a reasonable time and then checked inside the bank; there was a walk-through to another street. As sequel to this, when we got on the ship, where Mr. O'Brien was to be a fellow passenger, Jack kept a look out for him; his faith in the large gentleman was such that he kept inventing excuses for him and why he hadn't returned from the bank. To finally convince him, I suggested that he contact the purser and check the passenger list. There was no Mr. O'Brien on the Moreton Bay list.

Then there was the fellow migrant who had lost his wallet, a very sad deserving case, a poor lone Scot, no friends. We passed the hat around and we gave from our meager banks. He did all right, but his name wasn't on the ship list either. You live and learn; the education can sometimes be costly.

The SS Moreton Bay

One of the Commonwealth Government Line of passenger ships built to bring passengers from England. It was a turbine steamer built by Vickers, Barrow. It was 549 X 68.2 ft. Launched on April 23 1921 and completed on November 18. The maiden voyage was on December 7, 1921, Brisbane to London.

During the Second World War it was used as a troop transport. After the war it was put back into passenger service again, London to Sydney. In April of 1957 the ship was sold to be broken up at Barrow.

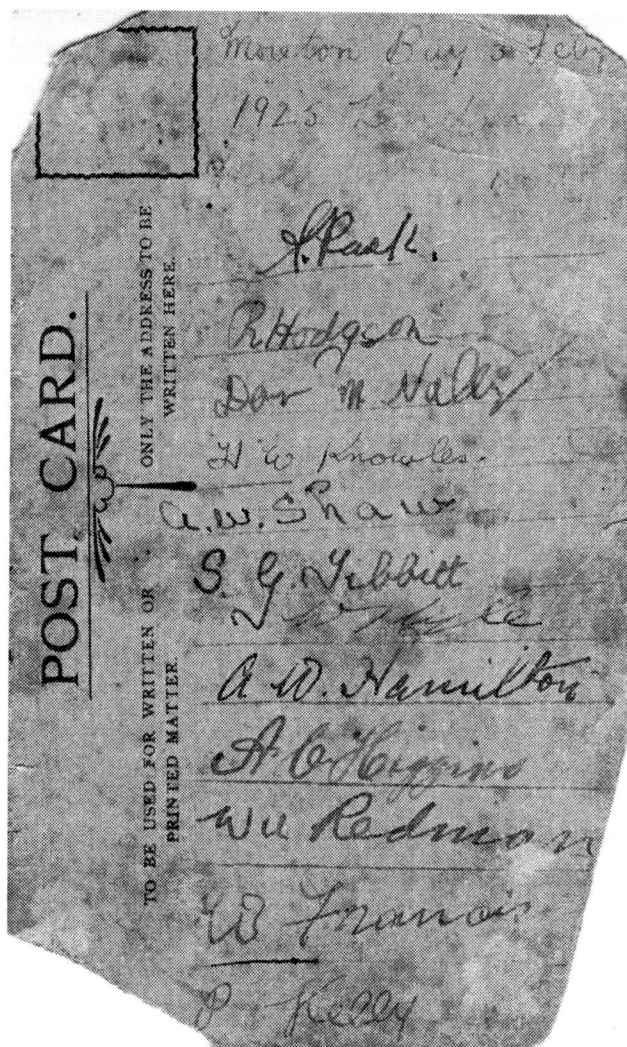

Back of SS Moreton Bay Postcard

The postcard is from Patrick Kelly's collection of memorabilia. The
names on the back of the postcard were at first thought to be of his
passenger mates on the voyage from England to Australia. Since that
time a search of the records of the passenger list of the SS Moreton Bay

indicates that only one name was a passenger. Does anyone in our reader audience recognize some of the names? These almost appear to be autographs.

CHAPTER TWO

On the morning of February 3rd, 1925, all was hustle and bustle as we left our temporary abode in Mills St. and headed for Euston Station en route to Tilbury docks. We had, as befitted our financial status, walked to the station, loaded with suitcases and baggage; it almost seemed we would never get there. It seemed we may have lost our way, so one of our party inquired of a chap leaning on a broom, if we were going right for the station. "Oh, no," he said. "You go that way," pointing to the opposite direction to where we thought the station ought to be. We took his advice only to be met further on by some of our acquaintances also bound for the ship, they too had been given the wrong direction. On returning we passed the person who had given us the wrong steer. He was laughing jeeringly; the other party noticed him too. He was either hostile to intending migrants or had a queer sense of humour. Our Scotty mate said, "Why did you give us the wrong direction?" "Bloody mugs," he said. With that the Scotty gave him a mighty wallop on the ear. "Maybe that will give you a better sense of direction." It must have hurt as we found out later that Scotty had been a middle weight champion boxer!

On arrival at Tilbury, we had a formal medical exam as we boarded the ship. The Moreton Bay was a unit of the Australian Commonwealth line of ships, a one class vessel where migrants and returning tourists mixed without restrictions imposed by the Class liners. The accommodation was good; I was extremely fortunate, perhaps my shipping agents had been good; funny, I can't correctly remember their names, but I think it was the Ridgeways. Anyway, I had eleven roommates in a fairly spacious cabin, on B deck, which was above the water line. The bunks were double decker and mine stretched across the two portholes so I could lie in bed and watch the scenery.

My roommates were a nice bunch of fellows, some were middle-aged and had families traveling on another part of the ship. What brought home to me how lucky I was, I thank my good agent again, I went below with one of my roommates to visit his family and found that some of the accommodations had been set up in cargo sections partitioned off to make sleeping quarters; these were of course below the water line. There was a stale musty smell and aromas of butter, cheese and ghosts of other cargoes haunted the area.

The air-conditioning was overtaxed and must have been barely tolerable in the tropics, which probably accounted for the many people who slept on the open decks. I remember one night, a hot steamy evening somewhere in the Red Sea, a sudden thunderstorm came up; it doesn't rain in those parts, the sky just opens up and old Jupiter unloads it in oceans of water.

My diary seems to show an unusual interest in the weather, days and dates records [ed], very hot, storms, and ever recurring, no land in sight. To a young person anxious to get to the end of the journey, and to get work, there was tedium. The sightseeing part would come later when I had made my fortune; there would in a few years be a grand tour, and I would see it all again.

Then of course there was a financial barrier. I recall my arrival at Port Said. I was hoping to go ashore; I had met a young Australian girl on board. She was returning from a tour and the Wembley exhibition. She asked me to escort her ashore, but being too proud to admit lack of finance and not willing to accept her help, I arranged for a young friend to escort her. That introduction, as I heard later, led to a wedding. So not wanting to show myself up as a liar, (I had pleaded illness), I now had to forego my trip ashore. The attractions, plenty - dozens of hawkers came aboard with all sorts of wares - genuine souvenirs of the East, made in Birmingham or Dublin. Then there were the youngsters diving for coins thrown into the water by the passengers.

I begrudged the time spent in port though it was fascinating. I was moved by the coolies at the coaling station; they worked like ants in a chain system, the worker scooped up his bucket of coal and went down a hatch in the ship's side to emerge at the tail of the chain again. The coal was brought alongside on a lighter and I was told that Port Said was one of the fastest coaling stations in the world. Not being one for statistics, that I have never questioned, but what I did question was the sight of those poor dust-grimed human beings worked like animals for a mere pittance; yet I suppose in years to come I was myself to suffer many insults to human dignity, as Tom Collins said, "such is life!"

My diary strangely makes no reference to our passing through the Suez Canal, but pass through we did. I did record being in the Indian Ocean and beautiful weather. On 24th February we were in Columbo Harbour; owing to some dispute over harbour dues our ship didn't berth at a quay; instead we were anchored at what I reckoned was two miles offshore. Cargo was loaded and unloaded from small boats and lighters. Passengers wanting to go ashore could board a small ferry, or take a chance of a ducking and travel on a small rowboat manned by an almost naked rower. My mate and I decided on the small rowboat chiefly because the fare was half that on the ferry. Arriving on the quay, we were besieged by money changers. We were however taken in tow by an authorized government guide. At least he showed us a badge of authority, and his main assistance, it seemed to me, was in taking us to certain shops and emporiums of his own choosing. We would have much more liked to do our own choosing, but he apparently considered himself our guardian angel. He didn't actually relate to any conception I had of an angel, he was a small brown man with a happy good humour, and his English was faultless. His feet were bare and the pavement must have really baked them. The sun was very hot and seemed to burn your very eyeballs. There was an acrid smell like stale urine, and cattle wandering through the traffic. I developed a headache.

We were constantly accosted by girls, and besieged by begging children. In spite of good advice from our guide, we gave a few coppers to the kids; we were over-run by little naked bodies. Our guard went into action, his horny bare foot connecting with little bare backsides were like rifle shots. Our guide had earned the pittance we could afford to give him.

One funny incident (from my point of view), my mate, Dan, decided that his uncovered head was not being improved by the sun, so to buy a new hat. Our guide knew the very place. There were plenty of hats but Dan was very fussy. As I mentioned earlier, Dan was at least ten years my senior; he had been around a bit, even had a spell in the Eire Army. His sense of humour was a little at variance with mine, but I suppose it was amusing to see the pile of tried-on hats growing, and the shop proprietor getting more edgy all the while. In a nervous burst he tried to help Dan decide by pulling the hat down hard on Dan's head - result - when they tried to get it off, it was stuck hard. The shop man ran around waving his arms, and his language, although we didn't understand it, seemed inflammatory.

It was Dan's turn to get a burst of energy. With the help of the guide, the hat finally separated from Dan's head minus the inside band which still adhered to Dan's head. I decided it was time I was somewhere else. Dan soon joined me minus a hat, and from the shop came a tide of vocal sound before the guide joined us. Somehow he steered us away from shops after that.

I ventured into a little shop near the quay to get some chewies - a little lady there detected an Irish accent and informed me she was an exile from Cork. There was a story there I'm sure, but it was time to join the ship again. Again we got in the little rowboat, this time a two-man power craft. We had not gone very far when a sudden squall came up. One minute the little craft was up in the air, and then it would bottom with a terrible jolt. The blinding rain made it impossible to see anything. I thought, this is it, I couldn't swim, and so it seemed very likely that my scraps of luggage would arrive in Australia without me. We were drenched, our oarsmen had no worries on that score, they were naked. One of them was now full-time baling water from the boat. We reached the ship but could not get close without being bashed to pieces on the ship's side, or crash on one of the lighters or cargo craft. Once, when close to a lighter, Dan got up and jumped onto it. I was rowed out again to ride it out from the other craft. Eventually we got back on board. I vowed then I would learn to swim, but I never really did.

Another incident that evening in Columbo Harbour - after the first storm was over, many passengers who had stayed on shore were caught in a second storm and then we, from the safety of the ship, watched them arriving on the ferry boat laden down with the spoils of shopping. Twice the ferry had to pull away as the ship was rising and falling; for the nimble there was no trouble but one lady of very ample proportions had several tries to get on the ship's gangway. Finally, having separated her from the piles of shopping, a couple of seamen got her within launching distance; another seaman was clinging on to the gangway to receive her. Somehow her legs failed to operate and she landed broadside. The seaman, working one handed, grabbed her, and with the upheaval of the ship, succeeded in landing her; we found out afterwards that the seaman's arm had been crushed between the ship's side and the gangway. Well, what have these instances to do with the story of a life time? My only excuse is, that they are part of memory, and our lives are packed with memories, happy or otherwise.

There was plenty of time to cogitate on the future as I already mentioned. I had an impatient urge to see the end of the voyage and start making a new life. Many of my shipmates were content to while the time away in the ship's canteen. Being tee-to-tal, this sort of thing had no attraction for me. The long stretches of ocean without sight of land became very boring; passing a distant island or ship was a matter of interest. The sight of another liner with lights ablaze at night was a beautiful sight.

CHAPTER THREE

On March 5th, a nice breezy day, flocks of birds appeared, which was a sign of nearing land, and the morning of the 6th, we awoke in Freemantle Harbour. Ashore at Freemantle, walking on land seemed queer. We were suffering from sailor's legs and the ground seemed to keep rolling. I liked Freemantle and wished that I were staying there. We had decided to visit Perth but one of our cabin mates who had his home in Perth arrived back at [the] ship with his three lovely sisters. Somehow Perth didn't seem so attractive any more. This gentleman had been visiting his birthplace as a freelance photographer. He had some interesting scenes of Wembley Exhibition which had been a big tourist draw in England. When he was not busy on the voyage with his camera, he slept. He was the sleepiest man I have known. It was farewell to Freemantle and all our good friends and at 11pm we headed out to the Southern Ocean. I always remember Freemantle as a friendly town. While visiting St. Pat's Cathedral, we were approached by a couple of our countrymen who had been in Australia for some years. They in turn introduced us to some other townspeople and we were invited to their homes and received offers of employment. However, the terms of our contract was [were] Victoria as our destination.

One point of interest during our walk around the port was a large sandstone quarry where the stone was cut by hand with saws and loaded on to horse drays. The stone cut easily into building blocks. One of the drays had been overloaded and had got bogged. The driver appealed to us to give a push off. So with the aid of six hefty bodies the horse with his overload was sent on his way. "I'll shout you all a beer if you come down to the pub," the driver called; however, we had better things to do, and so far I've never been able to get to see Freemantle since. But here's hoping, who knows?

We encountered an Englishman who had boarded at Freemantle bound for the eastern states, or, as they say, going up river! Anxious to bone-up on conditions, we started asking him questions. One of his statements intrigued me. According to his ideas, you went out into the bush, worked like hell for six months or so, got a bit of a bank, then back to the city for a bit of a booze up. I queried the idea of spending hard earned money on "grog." "Oh," he said, "You wouldn't last in this country if you didn't drink beer!" It seemed a bleak outlook for me; I was tee-to-tal but to this day, I've managed to exist without beer. That chap could have been in error.

On the evening of the 10th, we arrived at Port Adelaide which at that time was a rather dreary place. In port with us was a P & O Liner which had left London a week before us. The vessel, a migrant ship, had traveled by the Cape route. We were taken on board by a friend of one of our shipmates. The place was a shambles; taps had been left turned on, panels had been smashed in the bathrooms, linen and bedding were scattered all over the corridors. According to some of the migrant passengers, conditions on the voyage had been very bad. There were complaints about the food served, and gross overcrowding in some of the makeshift partitions in the converted cargo holds. Passengers leaving at Port Adelaide had made their feelings known. There had also been much sickness aboard and some migrants had been quarantined.

We realized then how fortunate we were to be on a good ship. The crew of the Moreton Bay were nearly all from the Northern Isles of Scotland. Perhaps, I should mention here that the Moreton Bay was one of a group of national liners known as the Commonwealth Line. This national asset was later disposed of to vested interests by a conservative government whose main slogan was private enterprise. A strong rumour, still alive, said that the Commonwealth was never paid for the ships.

At Port Adelaide we were besieged by groups of British migrants who had been brought here in previous years...some anxious for news of home, others apparently destitute, and all with stories of hardship. Some found their way aboard where they hoped to scrounge some food, and maybe borrow or beg from the crew; it was no use trying us for a handout, as finances were zero among the migrants. We heard very little good about Australia from these fellows who in the main were city boys - from the large British cities mostly.

I thought then what a miserable bunch of moaners, and passed them off as what is known in Australia today as "Whinging Poms." In my youthful arrogance, I was prepared to class them as no-hopers, not knowing at the time what a shock it must have been to a city-bred boy to find himself launched into the rough, often primitive conditions existing then on farms and large grazing properties. The then attitude to "new chums" as they were called, was a sort of veiled intolerance, and even some question as to the capacity of their intelligence. I doubt even now if the average Australian city boy were placed in similar circumstances that he would perform any better than the English city boy.

What I did find out later was a contributing factor to migrant problems in Adelaide, which caused me to re-orient my opinion of the boys we met at the port. What was later known as the Great Depression had already hit South Australia and not being an industrialized state there was much unemployment and men were crowding into the city hoping to find work. In the following year, a bunch of migrants headed for the eastern states were unloaded at Western Australia and dumped out in a camp far away from amenities and told if they showed up in the city they could find themselves in prison. Among this lot was a friend of mine who made his way to Victoria on foot; he is now a good Australian, but retains bitter memories of his initial reception.

CHAPTER FOUR

In case it is thought that because I remember and relate, perhaps with over-stress, incidents of my earlier years, that I am resentful of things that happened to me. Let me firstly state, I loved Australia from the first moment I set foot on its soil at Freemantle. I am an Australian with my roots firmly planted. But that has not blinded me to past faults, injustices and inequalities which exist even today.

From its inceptions as a white governed people, Australia has been plagued by petty tyrants and self-seeking go-getters, a minority, no doubt, but receiving an acceptance that today they may not receive elsewhere. We are inclined even today to give adulation to some of our earlier settlers who, if justice had been meted as it should, would have ended on the gallows. One such character has even been honoured by having his portrait inscribed on our currency.

What has history got to do with my life's story? Well, at the time of my arrival in Australia, the country was still young as far as the white settlers were concerned. Melbourne had not yet reached its centenary. There were still many who had taken part in the gold rushes. I consider that I took some part in helping to build Victoria. I was no pioneer, but I did assist in the forming and building of roads where none existed, clearing virgin brush, and putting down dams for water, only a small effort but one which increased my love for the fast disappearing Australian Bush.

But we are still on the ship, and at 5:30am on the 11th, March 1925, we said good-bye to Port Adelaide with no particular regret. The morning was quite cool. Some islands comprised the scenery and on the 12th March we came through the heads into Port Phillip Bay. Land was in sight on either side. We came into Victoria dock. There my skimpy diary comes to an end.

Emotions were tested when we watched the lucky people who had relatives to meet them - Australians returning after touring Britain and the Continent, and some lucky migrants whose relatives had preceded them.

I should perhaps make it clear here that we were not in the fortunate positions of those migrants who came here in later years, especially after World War II. We were on what was called an assisted passage, having promised to refund the Australian Migration Department the amount which was loaned to us for the fare. From memory I think it was about ninety pound sterling. We had already deposited an amount of landing money with the State Bank to ensure that we would have some funds until we found employment.

The later migrants came here on fares from ten pound [s] to twenty pounds each, and on arrival they were met and placed in hostels. These hostels were probably a bit of a shock to British migrants who had left good homes, but to refugees from the war-torn countries of Europe, they were at least equal to the shelters they had left.

I reimbursed the Migration Department my encumbrance within eighteen months.

One incident to recall - an elderly passenger missed his footing on the gangway and fell into the water. One of our group, a young Englishman, jumped in and brought him to the surface, the old man couldn't swim. The incident was reported in a new evening newspaper, *The Star*, and comment was made how the young man had to wait around in his soaked clothing till such time as his luggage was cleared by Customs.

On saying good-bye to the ship, five of us climbed into a horse-drawn cab and were taken to the junction of Flinders and Spencer Street which was as far as the horse drawn cab was allowed to operate. Acting on some good advice, we deposited our luggage at the Spencer Street Rail Cloakroom. On walking back via Flinders Street, I had a queer feeling that I had been here before. Even years later, this feeling still persisted. There is, I believe, a plaque on the footpath saying that John Batman landed on this spot. I am not even considering that my landing had any relation to John Batman's landing though I have heard that such feelings of previous experiences have been felt in various places by many people. Could be one of my ancestors landed with Batman.

We lost no time visiting the Migration Centre, then in Russell Street, where we were treated with every consideration. We were given an address where we were to stay in an [a] hotel not far from Spencer Street which was convenient as we were able to retrieve our luggage. The place was crowded. There was a Rifle Club competition and members from all over Australia were in Melbourne.

It was apparent that this was the transit accommodation for migrants as my roommate was an Irishman who had been detained for a week because his wife and family had been quarantined because of some fever. During the night I woke up with a severe itching. On turning on the light, I discovered hundreds of black insects crawling over the bed. I woke my roommate and asked him if he had any trouble. "By Hell," he said, "I have felt a bit itchy." He must have had a hide like an elephant. He said the things were bed bugs; I had never seen a beg bug before. I spent the rest of the night on the floor away from my bed. Just to prove how persistent the pests are, I found one in my suitcase when I got to my place of employment.

Anyhow, after spending a wretched night, I found the manager next morning and gave him a bit of my mind. He was apologetic and explained that because of the influx of visitors some spare rooms had been brought into use; I was unfortunate to get one of them. My roommate must have been a tough old boy; he had put up with it for days. I was shifted to better quarters. It was not a nice experience on my first night in Australia. Even though I thoroughly disinfected and scrubbed in the bath, I would still itch for days. I have slept in many strange beds and places since that night but that was my worst experience.

Next morning we went to explore the city. It was a Saturday and we were informed there was to be a St. Patrick's Day march. Being Irish it was assumed we would be interested. I said I was more interested in some green scenery, so after some inquiry, we found ourselves in maybe the Botanical or the Alexander Gardens, and after weeks on the ocean it was an earthly heaven. In my scruffy little diary, there is still the imprint of a flower I picked and pressed there on that very morning.

The weather was perfect and had it not been for the urge to get settled into a job and get some money in our pockets we would have been happy to stay in Melbourne. I may say here that there was no possibility of getting a job in Melbourne. We had no skills which could help us. Though we were unaware of it then, the seeds of the Depression had already been sown, but more of that later.

CHAPTER FIVE

On the Monday morning, we assembled at the Migration Centre for an interview with their employment officer. Two jobs were available on wheat farms in the Mallee country some 200 miles from Melbourne. One farmer had an Irish name so I took that. Dan took the other which was a few miles closer to the town of Sea Lake. We were told we should have our own blankets, towels, etc. Wage 25 shillings a week and keep.

Our business concluded at the Centre, which included arrangements for travel, we went to the State Bank in Swanston Street and collected our money, then proceeded to shop for what things we would need. From memory I paid ten shillings for a stout pair of work boots, 25 shillings for blankets. I invested in a sewing kit for clothing repair, the remains of which I still have. A first-aid kit was advisable. So when all was finished there was very little left in my purse.

It scares me a little now to think of the faith I had in myself, heading off to an unknown destination in an unknown country with ten shillings in my pocket. Possibly I would have had more than a little unease if I had known then some of the conditions which existed for farm workers at that time; there was then no paid holidays, no sick pay, no proper worker's compensation, worker's hours were from sunrise to sunset six days a week and horses to be cared for on Sundays. In the winter time one struggled around with a hurricane lamp feeding and preparing the team for the day's work.

Dan and I traveled together to our proposed place of employment. We had to break our journey at Bendigo and we had a couple of hours to wait for our train to Sea Lake and Nandaly. I think the line ended at Kulwin. I liked Bendigo and still do. It was a mining city and at that time some gold mining was still going on. It interested me to know that in the 1850's and 60's all this country has [d] been the centre of a feverish search for gold; towns had sprung up everywhere. Life was rough and the country was as wild as the miners who flocked to it. Most of those towns are hamlets today. Some have vanished leaving only the turned earth and digger holes. Only the Chinese left lasting marks in the form of a little cultivated clearing, and some of their fruit trees still survive. Most of the others vanished like a whirlwind. Bendigo survived and is to my mind a beautiful city.

On that day in 1925, I was not in the mood for much sight-seeing; my impatient urge was still with me. The desire and the need to secure some cash drove me on. Aboard the train again we soon left the city behind. The scenery was changing; the country around was becoming free of the Whipstick Mallee and Sheoaks; it was now open wheat country and we could see in the distance clouds of dust which meant that horse teams were at work fallowing the land.

Being farm reared I got into conversation with my fellow travelers who explained the system of farming to me. Wheat, they told me was the main product. The land was ploughed and worked all through the season before planting. This was called fallowing and was intended to conserve the moisture in the soil, at the same time killing off germinating weeds. The expected rainfall, they explained, was only about 12 inches annually.

As we proceeded it was near nightfall; unlike the old country there was no twilight, they told me. As the dark came down I could see the glow of lots of fires on the horizon. Were they bush fires? I had heard something about the peril of Australian bushfires. I was told that the farmers were burning off. After the wheat crop was stripped, the remaining straw was burnt off; this was supposed to kill off any disease such as rust, smut or other pests. Another point was that it clogged up the ploughs and feeding machines. I ventured to say that in my way of farming, the process was to return as much straw and roughage as possible to restore humus, and to help bind the loose earth.

Now my friends in Ireland who had lived in Australia for some years informed me that one mortal sin that was not forgiven in Australia was to question or to give any advice on anything, which would imply that we knew anything about anything. If they do happen to accept any given advice, they claim it as their own. Well, I was only an Australian in the making in those days. However, on this particular point, when the Mallee country started to erode and drift in later years and was coating the country with red dust which penetrated into southern areas, saner councils prevailed, and a different type of farmer has now taken over.

I recall my new employer setting me a job of cutting down a shelter of Mallee trees, because, he said, wheat did not grow within a few yards of them, besides they were a shelter for the birds. I ventured, against my previous advice, that it might be wiser to plant a few more trees rather than destroy the existing ones. But in those days, it was said, most farmers carried an axe in their hip pocket. Be that as it may, terrible damage was done in many parts of Australia by the farmers' urge to denude areas which later suffered from erosion. Some of the naked water-torn hillsides in Gippsland today bear witness.

Conservation in those days had not been heard of. With few exceptions the early farmers were little different from the miners or gold diggers. Their motto seemed to be - get as much as you can out of the land and get out. More acres and more wheat. It could be that I was doing them some injustice as my inherited type of farm was much different, but after all those years I still think my assertion was right.

CHAPTER SIX

Perhaps I am cutting too wide a swathe. We are still on the train steaming slowly through the night. Our fellow passengers were a friendly lot; one old gentleman, of English origin to me, was a bachelor farmer around Charlton way, gave me his address and said, "If you strike it rough up there you can come and stay at my place until you get settled." Another middle-aged man wearing a turban, a former native of India, I forget the exact state, but he said he was now an Australian farmer, also gave us his address if we needed a friend or a holiday...look him up. We got a lot of good friendly advice.

The Indian gentleman was consuming a large bag of grapes which he offered to all. His method of eating was to crush a large handful of grapes in his mouth and separate the pips. In the centre of the carriage was a hole in the floor with a brass surround; this was the cuspidor or the spittoon. Our Indian friend would eject the mouthful of pips in the direction of the cuspidor, not all reached their mark.

Then there was another old wiry looking bushman with a beard stained with the juice of tobacco which he chewed; every so often he would lean over and let fly at the cuspidor. He often missed too. We were truly among rough men in a rough country. Still, I've traveled since then in much worse company. They were a friendly lot and unlike some of our country trains today, there were no beer cans or empty bottles rolling around.

One by one as we passed each stop, our passengers got off. We reached Sea Lake where I parted with Dan. Myself and two others were all that were left. On into the darkness with still an occasional glimpse of burning stubble. The air was still and warm and smelled of smoke and a peculiar dusty smell which I learned to relate to the Mallee. I must have dozed off. I awoke with one of the men shaking me, "This is yours, mate," he said. I sleepily gathered up my belongings and stepped out into the night. I felt myself tumbling into space, rolling down an embankment. The platform was about one carriage long and I had been at the rear of the train. It was dark, close to midnight. I saw a glimmer of light in the distance, so gathering up my cases and kit, I made my way towards it. Dropping my outfit I looked around, a small kerosene lamp hanging on a shed wall glimmered in the darkness. I heard some voices then. I saw some forms beside a couple of cars. So I walked up and asked if anyone knew Mr. M., [Dan Molone], who was to be my employer.

One man replied that they hadn't set eyes on him that night, then another fellow came along and we asked him if Mr. M. had been around; he said he thought Mr. M.'s car was down in the scrub and maybe he was over at the station attendants house collecting his mail. Mr. M. finally emerged out of the darkness. He was surprised when I introduced myself. "God's truth," he said, "I've got no news of you coming. I was only here by chance to get the mail." Well, one black mark to some clerk in the Migration Office, where I was told that I would be met at the Station.

"All right, get your gear," Mr. M. said, "It's a fair drive." Horror! When I went back to the shed to get my luggage, it was submerged in a crawling wave of mice, the place literally moved with them. I found they had nibbled holes in my cases. I even found some inside next day. A mouse plague, Mr. M. informed me, they occur every twenty years or so. Well, they had reduced a large stack of bagged wheat at the rail siding to a tumble down mess. Silos were only in their infancy in most areas. Later on this provided work for a few men, cleaning up and rebagging.

MOUSE PLAGUE

Now Rabbi Burns, guid man,
Would nae been half sae caring,
Had he here in the Mallee been
With these wee beasties sharing.
"Och aye" a wee and timid beastie,
"That may be!"
But try to live with them and see.

They foul our clothing
They foul our food,
An everlasting swarming brood.
And when it's night and time to rest
It's then they put us to the test.
They scratch our feet and bite our hair
Mice in bed and everywhere.

They say that for some monstrous vice
The Lord has plagued us with these mice.
"Boy" life in the Mallee must be grim
"How can we live with so much sin."
Well? Whatever! Who can tell?
We may be living on the edge of Hell!

~ P.K. ~

(Rabbie Burns wrote Ode to a Mouse)

(My first introduction to the Mallee in 1925 was greeted with hordes of
mice which damaged much of my clothing and belongings).

Eventually, after a drive which necessitated me hopping out to open several gates, we arrived at a cluster of buildings. The car, I noted, was an Overland and now and again seemed to have some gear difficulty. I was very tired. This is it, Mr. M. said, you have your blankets, there is a stretcher on the verandah, you can bed down for the night. It was after midnight; I was choking with thirst and I hadn't eaten since we left Bendigo. I suppose those problems didn't occur to Mr. M. He was probably tired too. So I spread my blankets and in spite of the mice crawling on the roof, I must have slept well. I was brought from slumber by something falling on my face and a furious screeching; a funny looking bird was perched on the bed over my head. It was a pink Galah but I had no name for it then. And I had never heard a bird screeching, "Who are you! Whoooooo."

At the bottom of the bed was another bird, a girl, I assumed about my own age, a small dark-haired girl. She was laughing her head off. She probably got a surprise to get up and find a strange man in the house. The girl informed me she was getting breakfast and it would soon be ready. Well, it couldn't be too soon for me. I felt stiff and sore from my stumble at the rail station, but I felt much better after breakfast. It was a beautiful morning and my Boss asked me if I wanted to start work that morning. I said, "Of course, I came here to work. Why should I not start today?" "Well," he said, "seeing that it's St. Patrick's Day, I thought you may want to celebrate." I then realised indeed it was St. Patrick's Day.

My first job was to have a look at my living quarters. It was not a very heartening sight, a small hut surrounded by an open galvanized roof shed. This shed was used as an implement shelter. The hut was occupied by a colony of fowls. A couple of Chooks were in the hatching process. The only furniture was the remains of a wire stretcher bed. I set to a general clean up...evicting the fowls, and with the aid of an army of children who had emerged from the house, we managed to transfer the broodys to a safe place. With the aid of an improvised bucket and a bottle of Jeyes fluid [a detergent and antiseptic] from my kit, I did my best to disinfect and make things uncomfortable for an army of spiders, large and small.

Then there was the problem of the mice. To combat these, I cut two shields from a Kero tin and fitted them to wire strung across the roof. The mice circumvented these more by dropping from the rafters on to whatever possessions I hung up. I had a good suit ruined as they ate holes in it. On with the restoration of my living room, there was no bedding, straw was out of the question because of the mice, so I got a large wool pack and filled it with Mallee leaves from the nearby bush, to serve as a mattress. Next I got four large glass jam jars half full of water and placed my bed legs in them making sure the bed was well clear of the walls where the vermin could creep up.

In those days farm supplies of lighting and motor fuel came in four-gallon cans packed in pairs in strong pine cases. The cases were well made and easily adapted for seating, cupboards, tables, or storage uses. Many a pioneer home and shacks were furnished with these sturdy cases. So with a bit of scrounging around the sheds, I soon had sufficient furniture for my needs. Unfortunately, I had human pests to contend with, in the shape of two small boys of the family. There was no lock on my door and during my absence they ransacked my belongings destroying several small relics I had brought from home. A beautiful razor blade was blunted and rendered useless. The strap, a present from my father, was slashed to pieces. Nothing much to worry about you may think, but to someone whose worldly possessions were contained in one small suitcase little things meant a lot.

There were eight children in the family, the oldest a girl my own age, another girl grown up, the oldest boy, Ed, was one year younger than I was. We became friends right off. They were a good family and treated me as one of them. The farm had been a run down, rabbit infested wilderness, but with hard work, Mr. M. was gradually knocking it into shape. I settled into work well enough, after all, driving an eight-horse team was not that much different from a two-horse team, and running a straight line of fence posts was no problem. Most of the fencing on the place was in a bad condition and needed general replacement. The horse team which I was allotted, I found in very poor condition. Their shoulders had been neglected, and much of the harness was ill-fitting. They were old timers in most cases, some were outlaws, but I supposed in Mr. M.'s position he couldn't afford first class horse flesh.

I loved horses and started right off to clear up their sores and trim their overgrown hooves. In spite of my efforts it was irritating driving a team barely equal to the effort required of them. Like thousands of exiles before me, I was homesick. I had lost my mother a year before leaving but I missed my father and brothers and sisters. As I have said, I was included in the family in my new home, but sometimes in the night I would get a heart searing loneliness. It wasn't so bad when I was busy, in fact sometimes I wished that I could work all night. On those occasions I dreaded coming to the hut. Gradually, however, I made outside friends and started to merge in.

In those days a letter took six weeks to get overseas and another six weeks for a reply, providing, of course, that your correspondent replied straight away. My father was very good. He wrote regularly. My sisters were poor correspondents. I had been some weeks on the farm without meeting anyone outside the family. One day while up on the windmill stand, I saw another farm house in the distance. "Hooray," I thought, there is someone only a couple of miles away. Imagine my disappointment when I was told the farm was deserted.

The season went around, cropping was completed and winter fallowing was well in hand. Our main worry was water. Water was not then laid on internally to the house. It was stored in two large galvanised iron tanks and these were replenished by rain off the roof. Rain was slow in coming and if you wanted some water from the tanks Mrs. M. carried the key in her pocket, because the young fry, like all children, were likely to leave the tap dripping, and precious water would be lost. It was a sort of religion to knock on the tanks every few days to see how many rims were left. Think of that all you city housewives of today, with washing machines, dishwashers, and hot water in the bath.

Stock water was brought in open channels from large reservoirs in the Grampians Range. It was a tortuous system, eighty percent of the water leeched away into the sand on its journey to the Mallee. It was, however, the life blood of that fertile but dry land. The water was delivered into dams or earth water tanks by small channels made on the farm. If the farmer was lucky, he might get a second top off before the flow was shut off the main channel. Drifting sand was a serious problem and in most cases the channel had to be cleared of sand drift before the water started to leave the main reservoir. Mr. M. who was a bit of a battler had some contracts for this work of sand clearing, so we had some hectic work at times. We did a bit of road clearing too. Roads in Northern Victoria in those days were just earth tracks with an occasional Mallee stump projecting. Many an unwary motorist had his sump or undercarriage torn while traveling in the dark, or on unknown roads. Henry Ford must have had the Mallee roads in mind with his early models, they were stump jumpers with good road clearance.

CHAPTER SEVEN

It may be that I am spending too much effort relating events, which, after all, were a very small dot in my lifetime, but it was a cataclysmic experience in my life. For that reason events of that period are more securely etched in my memory than experiences of later years. And further to that, the period between the two wars was unique in Australia.

The 1920's is an age now looked on by two later generations as an era of Romance - the "Roaring Twenties" they called it, but believe me most of the "roaring" was groans of frustration from the then younger generation, and the rising anger of a generation of men a little older than myself who had set out to war with the promise of a brave new world. Frustration, anger and insecurity. [!] Let us acknowledge that for the returned men some effort was made to settle them on the land, but there were more failures than successes, and a lot of serious effort and struggle went down the drain because of wool-brained planning.

One good intention carried to extreme was the Preference of returned men. This was prolonged so far that young men were being denied the jobs of their choosing by preference to their own fathers. I was too young to go to war yet on several occasions I was denied a job because someone older had preference. I'm not opposed to the Preference System, but it was allowed to outlive its purpose.

(I'm not sure if these digressions have any relation to my story, so I will try to run a straight furrow.)

Getting back to the farm, I got a pleasant surprise on weekend to get a call on the party line phone from my mate Dan; he was on a farm about four miles away, having been lent by his Boss to help a neighbour. By the way, a neighbour was anyone within twenty miles or so. (Digressing again.) "Happy Day." We arranged to meet on Sunday and we did, I with some friends, and a few boys with Dan. Quite a party, all carrying shotguns, which was not such bad news for the rabbits as you may think, because I'm afraid some could not hit the proverbial haystack. In the course of our afternoon forage, I had wounded a rabbit and not wanting to waste a further shot, I put my gun down, slipped through a fence and just got close enough to reach out for bunny when he disappeared in a cloud of fur and dust. It happens all the time, some idiots just can't be trusted with firearms...The young Englishman's excuse for nearly blowing my arm off was that he thought the rabbit might have got away. Dan, myself and my friend Bertie, decided that the party was too big and put some distance between us.

I've not introduced Bertie before; he worked on a neighbouring farm, a young Australian, we had become good friends. "Burlington Bertie" we called him. He was a very natty dresser. Just to show how frivolous youth can be, Bertie used to visit me.

Burlington Bertie [Bert Phillips] (c. 1926)

I think perhaps two nice girls might have been more reason; anyhow on his visits, Bertie always managed to get invited to stay for tea. Sitting down to tea one evening Bertie nudged me; on the floor the Galah which I have already introduced, was busy tearing a hat to pieces. Bertie whispered, "Watch him tearing the old man's hat to pieces." When it was time to go, Bertie, who had sported a nice new Borsalina hat, looked around where he had hung it. You guessed it!

Another Bertie episode. Ed took us for a drive in a horse drawn junker to see a small vineyard near the shores of Lake Tyrell which is a 25 mile long salt water lake. At that time salt was harvested on Lake Tyrell by piling it into heaps with horse drawn scoops, then it was shoveled into sacks for transport. The salt harvest provided some short time employment for casual workers. But we were going to see the vineyard. I had not seen grapes growing so I was interested. When we came within sight of a tumble down dwelling, we stopped. The owners of the vineyard were an aged hermit-like couple. There were down among the vines a couple of scarecrows presumably to keep the birds away from the fruit. Bertie aimed his gun at one of the figures, "Watch me blow it's hat off," he said. Just as he was about to fire, Eddie knocked the muzzle up. "You stupid cow," he said, "that's old Jake and his missus." Motto here. I believe that all carriers of firearms should be tested for competence. I've witnessed it happen many times...place a firearm in the hands of a seemingly sane person and he immediately wants to let loose at any visible target. Just note notice boards and signs on country roads and reserves and they invariably look like a sieve.

CHAPTER EIGHT

A highlight on the farm was the arrival after harvest (note the "after harvest" - that's when some reward was received for the year's labour) of a player piano complete with a library of music rolls of the latest hits. It may seem strange to the youth of today with their "Hi Fi" and music laid on in the car, and even in the toilet. In my day radio was in its infancy; T.V. was still a dream on the ether.

Some people in favoured reception areas did have some sort of battery receivers, such innovations had not yet reached our part of Victoria. The piano was like an oasis in the desert. Weekends, the home would be packed with people. I had the pleasure of teaching the girls the latest dance steps. Ely danced like a fairy, Mady was a little difficult, the other girl, Kit, started to feel grown-up too. Someone produced a fiddle, I managed to inject a few Irish tunes among the hits...songs like *Lily of Laguna*, *Don't Bring Lulu* and *Barney Google* and many First World War favourites rattled off the old player. I suppose in some places they are still treasured relics.

To improve our social life, Ed and I spent several weekends grading and fencing a tennis court; result that when our non-working hours arrived the court would be packed with females; we just never got a look in. When I mention weekends that only meant Sunday. Saturday was a full working day. About one Sunday in three we would go to Mass in a little hall about five miles away. The hall was used as a holy place by at least four denominations. On some very important church event, we would go into town for the service.

It was a torrid morning on the Mass day; imagine five adults and five or six youngsters all trying to pile into the Overland. Someone was always found to be minus a shirt or a shoe. On one demoralizing trip, two ladies had forgotten their unmentionables. That news leaked through the younger fry who were happy to know that grown-ups make mistakes too. We had a mission in town and the preacher must have been a relation of Billy Graham. Ed and I were unfortunately seated in the front row. The fire and brimstone from the pulpit seemed to hover directly over us. It was a real old time sermon and was seemingly infinitive, but it did end, and even now recalling it after fifty odd years, there is grave doubt, taking that sermon as a yardstick that there is any hope for the vast majority, especially Catholics. The rest of humanity had no hope from the start!

Coming out from church I noticed Ed had a grey stricken look and he was trembling a bit. It wasn't a cold evening, so I said, "What's wrong Ed? Are you all right?" "All right!" he said, "did you see him? Every time he lifted his hand he pointed at me and looked directly at me. It will be a long time before I go to a mission again." Ed was emerging into manhood and the pressures and passions of adult life were surging. Like myself, he had led a sheltered life and if we had any education on sex, it was probably fallacious and ill-informed. According to our preacher to acquire or entertain questions of sex in your mind was inviting, "Hell's fire and direct damnation." It was a very chastened group of girls and boys who set off back to the farm.

A big programme of fencing was in the offing, so the Boss reckoned we would have to get a supply of fence posts, and the least costly way to get them was to cut and cart them. So one morning bright and early, I set off with a wagon drawn by an eight-horse team. It was twelve miles to town and we had another ten or twelve miles to the forest reserve. The Boss said, "I'll meet you in town at the rail station," which he did. There he had scrounged a large tarpaulin which was to be my shelter. I had a supply of chaff feed for the horses.

The idea was, the Boss and another fellow cut the posts which would be loaded onto the wagon. I was then to take them to an arranged spot on the way to town. It was not possible to get all the way to the rail and get back in time to get loaded again for the next day. A motor truck was to carry them the remaining miles to the railyard. My first task on arrival in the forest was to string a barb wire corral to contain my team, then a rope stretched between two trees made a support for my improvised tent. Inside I stacked all the chaff. The mouse plague by this time was as if it had never been; the horses were on their feed again, they had turned off their chaff when it was mouse infected. Feeders made from sacks or wool packs were stretched between the saplings. I then gathered my team and proceeded to the cutting area where I was loaded and drove on to a firm track ready for an early start in the morning.

The sun was setting; the Boss and his offsider passed me on the way out. I took my horse to a drink at the waterhole, then off to camp. I was just sitting down in the light of a hurricane lamp when it struck me...the loneliness of the bush. Here I was, not six months in the country, sitting alone in a timber area, not knowing where my nearest neighbour was. The night set in with possums hissing in the trees. Away down by the waterhole I could hear a Plover, then the Mopoke started. I could hear my horses stamping and snorting over their feeders. As I started in on the prepared meal the Boss had left me, I thought of the pioneers who came to this great strange beautiful country and I thought of the women, those brave hardy women, often alone when their husbands were away for long periods. Their courage had helped to bring this country to maturity. I then wondered about the Australian women of my generation, the girls on the farm for instance, would they be equal to their grandmothers?

I had determined not to get enmeshed in any romances until such time as I was independent. In my youthful arrogance, I had yet to learn we are not masters of our destiny. It is strange how I can still recall with clarity even my very thoughts on certain occasions. Some experiences come to be part of your very being.

Tired, so after tea I checked the horse yard, all seemed secure. I rolled a couple of bags of chaff, spread my blankets, laid the sharp axe by the bedside and turned in. This was not a place for silk pyjamas even had I owned such. I must have slept and woke with a start, the tarp was moving, I grabbed an axe. Now I know that men since then have slept in holes in strange jungles, my brother among them, with their rifles beside them, and it is possible they have had the same flutter of pulse that I felt then. The bag of chaff started to move from under the tarp. I sprang out. There was the culprit. One of my horses must have felt his ration was not sufficient and had come for a self serve. I grabbed the mane and escorted the animal back, let down the wire inlet and put him or her inside. Shadows moved in the dark aisles among the trees, the moonlight was fleeting. Something suggested that I should count the heads, there were nine, I only had eight. Here was a quandary; if I left the stranger, could be I'd find a horse with a broken leg or something in the morning, because horses like humans do fight sometimes. On the other hand, some of my team I was not very familiar with, as I had sort of picked a team for the job from among all the horses on the farm. So I just bided around and tried to remember who had white stars, who had a white stocking, which were mare, which were gelding. When I finally worked it out, I made my pick, took the offender out of the corral. Here was a hard decision if I just gently patted him good-bye more than likely he would return in my absence and clean up the feed that was to do my team for two weeks. On the other hand his crime had been a natural instinct to help himself to feed that was there to be taken. I love horses but sane reasoning had to be obeyed, so I picked up a nice waddy and applied it to his rump enough to frighten the bedamnits out of him. I listened to the echo of his hooves on the hard earth for some time. He never came back.

Dreamtime By A Campfire

Quietly and brightly the campfire is burning,
And strange are the pictures I see in the glow,
Across the tall tree tops deep shadows flicker,
And join with the images I see as they go.

The friendly eucalyptus bend to receive them
No goblins here with their evil spleen,
I'm as one with the nights and quiet bush setting
No wood nymph abroad to disturb the scene.

But hark in the shadows a rustle of leather
The clink of stirrups come faintly to ear.
Yes, those phantom troopers they still go riding
Chasing bush rangers who roamed around here.

But the bushrangers are gone and so are the troopers,
Could have been a hunter stalking a 'roo,
So thus I sat and silently pondered
But there in the shadows the images grew.

A bullock team lumbered away to the diggings
And diggers passed by in a motley array
A cavalcade screened by smoke through the trees
Can it be Burke and Wills passing this way?

A mopoke was paging his mate in the tree tops
And to add a weird note the curlew's loud shriek,
Afar through the shadows a campfire gleaming,

Must be a swagman down by the creek.

The dew of the morning shone bright on the myrtle,
A magpie's loud carol to bid me good-day,
The campfire's bright glow, now smothered in ashes
My friends of the night now seemed far away.

Visions, dreams, or charms of the bushland,
Do we need a reason to tell them apart,
And though I may strive in a city's confinement
The lure of the bushland is etched in my heart.

~P.K. 1/10/82~

That stint of work ended with me working half the night to arrive home slipping and sliding all over the track in pouring rain. The rain was welcome and so was the home; you know it just seemed like home to me now. One little incident I overlooked. The Boss had picked up a young fellow from the city; there was a strike in there, he was able to help me load, and a bit of company for me. One night was enough. It was dark. Suddenly he ran up to me, "There's a woman screaming away down there!" he said. I said, "You have never heard a curlew?" Being city-bred he never had; the curlew's cry is really weird and did sound a bit eerie in the forest. One night would be enough for me here he said, if I got ten pounds a night. He went off with the Boss the next evening.

Our, or rather my next job, was to load the posts at the home railyard and bring them to the farm. A handyman who was doing some repairs to the home was detailed to help me at the station. I only include this incident because it sheeted home to me how vulnerable the bush worker can be unless he has some money behind him. My assistant was not a young man and without making too harsh a judgment, the name "handyman" could not be taken literally. He was a bungler. He was also an ugly Australian, a species which, thank God, is almost extinct. He seemed to have an ingrained opposition to anyone who was not born here, at the same time lauding his Anglo-Saxon ancestry, maybe too he didn't like Irishmen, especially those who didn't knuckle under. In the process of unloading, I asked him to steady a large post while I moved to receive it on the wagon. Like the bungler he was, just as I reached for it, he pushed. I went down on the wagon rail with two hundred weight of timber across my chest. Well, I suffered agony with my ribs for weeks, then I thought what would have happened had I broken a leg or my spine. No compensation, no sick pay. While Christian ethics might have invited my employer to care for me, economic circumstances would have, more likely, shoved me off into the bleak world of reality. Whatever, this mishap fired my urge to make my bank a sufficient buttress for my future well-being. Only those who have cast off from family and friends will fully understand my motivation. When there is no one to turn to for a helping hand the world can seem very bleak. Maybe my close family upbringing had rendered me more vulnerable and my feeling of aloneness may have been unique.

When first I left old Ireland's shore
The yarns that we were told.
Of how folks in far Australia
Could pick up lumps of gold.
How gold dust lay in all the streets
and miners' rights were free
Hurrah I told my loving friends
That's just the place for me.
~ Anon(ymous) ~

CHAPTER NINE

I was now approaching twelve months in Australia. I hadn't yet found any gold, but I was starting to assimilate and take an interest in the affairs of the nation. An election was in the offing, so the Boss explained to me how to get on the electoral roll, and the particular party to vote for, pointing out also that such a party was more sympathetic to the Catholic minority. I thought, "My God, surely not here!" Not the eternal bigotry and sectarian bickering which had been a cancer in the heart of my country for countless years, a bigotry which I may aver, prevented myself from gaining a job in any but the most manual employment. May be that some things should be unsaid, but I had an aversion to bigotry under any disguise. I did some boning up on the elections and came to my own conclusions.

About that time the population of Australia was between six and seven million people. I discovered that the main purpose for bringing in migrants was not nation building; they were needed as a source of cheap labour for the farmers as most Australians preferred to work in the city where there was a semblance of a wage and conditions justice. The farm or country workers, with the exception of a pastoral award which protected shearers, were Cinderellas without any set conditions to protect them.

I resolved it was time for a change. My friend Jack, who had been working in the Gippsland area wrote me, and being of the same mind we thought to pool our money and buy a team and go contracting. There was a bit of work road-making and drainage in the new closer settlement areas (Nar Nar Goon) which were being developed by the state government. However, as the poet Burns wrote, "The best made plans of mice and men aft gang aglay." Such was our case. Jack, who was working for a contractor, had shifted to some unknown camp. Huge bushfires were raging. The small town of Bunyip where I was put up was shrouded in smoke. I felt hemmed in; after the open Mallee country I felt oppressed. Maybe working in Gippsland wasn't my cup of tea. I went back to Melbourne. I tried to see if there was any chance to learn a trade.

I was then 21...too old they said. But one bit of information seemed brighter. If I could get some sort of a job in or near the city, I could go to night school at the Melbourne Tech. I tried every avenue, the Tramways, the Railways and various factories. Next I canvassed the rural areas next to the city. This was orchard and market gardening country (around Moorabbin and Bentleigh). Not a hope. So I fronted up at the government labour exchange to inquire about country work.

In the twelve months with Mr. M., I had done dam sinking, road work, and was proficient at all farm work. I should perhaps mention here that Mr. M. had offered me to work on a share in the crop basis. That would have meant a minimal wage and a gamble on the coming wheat crop of which I would have a percentage. Not being a gambler, I was not inclined to take the punt. I knew Mr. M. himself was on one big gamble.

Thinking over it now, I believe probably I wanted to be in control of my own destiny. Had I taken the offer I would have felt tied. He had asked me to give the city a try and come back if I wanted. After failing to find work in the city, I suppose pride among other reasons would not let me go back.

The man in the Labour Bureau was very helpful. I had expressed a desire to get to the Mildura district which was a young settlement on the way up. He told me there was job at Rainbow, two pounds a week and keep. It sounded pretty good as I had said that I wanted at least two pounds. There was one drawback, on the evidence of some men who had gone there from the Bureau - the farmer was a proper old bastard. In fact, the man who had vacated the job would be in on the morning. I could get all the facts on the set up if I liked to meet him next morning.

I met the chap next morning, a very competent Scotchman. He explained to me that the supposed Boss was the old man's son, but the old fellow kept interfering all the time. I took the job. The old boy was two old bastards rolled into one; I stayed six months. I had been reading a history of Australia and he reminded me of the old tyrant Marsden, the flogging parson. Well, this old boy didn't flog, but he would have liked to. I remember our final parting when I told him what I thought of him. He spluttered, "you bloody Poms are all the same." I informed him firstly I was not a Pom, and secondly if I died in Australia next week, I would get six feet of Australia the same as he would. He was a disgrace to his Scotch ancestors.

I had made a good friend on the job. Les was a Sydney born boy of French ancestry. He owned a nice motor bike which was very handy and we had many trips together. I had some money saved and was about to buy a late model motor bike, but a mishap on a slippery road changed my mind. I never had any cause to reverse my decision about motor bikes. When Les learned on a Sunday morning that I was pulling out, he said, "Wait till I get my money and I'll be with you." We both prepared to head for town on Les's steed. When the fellow who was supposed to be Boss found out he was losing two men, he rushed to us and asked us to reconsider. We told him when you can control the old boy you will have more luck with your workers. That was life in the Bush, you win a few, you lose a few. But sometimes human dignity takes a bashing in the meantime.

CHAPTER TEN

The six months spent on this job had many lonely boring times. The holdings consisted of three farms. We had three teams, and the set up of work was such that one team worked for a period on the home farm while the other two worked as a pair away. I was the one out. On their return it would be my turn to go to the Outpost farms. Then there would be long lonely days and nights without company, no radio or T.V. in those days. My meals would be delivered to the house on the farm during my absence in the paddocks. It became very boring. I often thought about the story of the Hatters who would place their hat on a post and have a conversation. Occasionally Les would come of a Sunday and take me for a spin on his bike.

One fine summer's day we went for a trip to Lake Hindmarsh, a large fresh water lake. This was a great picnic area for visitors from miles around. The day we arrived was Gala Day. Les being a bit of a show-off roared down through the sand to the water's edge; unfortunately, his brakes missed out on the loose sand. We finished up with the bike up to our necks in water, to the great glee of many of the onlookers. Well, we were young, we could even laugh at ourselves.

We had booked in at a friendly hotel in Rainbow. We had been there a couple of days when Les was offered a job not far from the one we just left. I was just mooching around, when the hotel man, who knew I was open for employment, introduced me to a man who was looking for someone. He was a farmer from down Nhill way, just up visiting relations. Yes, I was looking for a job I explained to him but I was trying to get away from farm work. He seemed a decent easy sort of fellow. He told me if I came with him and helped him with his extra work I may be able to get something to suit me. He had a friend who was a contractor, roadwork, etc., and if I was not satisfied with the farm job, he would put in a word for me to his friend. I took the job, £2 a week and keep, so off we went down to Nhill.

I was made welcome by the lady of the house, and for the first time I was given a room in the house and treated as one of the family. The lady even offered to do my washing. In return I did a spot of baby sitting when they wanted an evening out. There was a baby and a boy of three. I was really one of the family and we had many social outings. However, I still had the hankering to get away from farm work. One day Norm, my Boss [Norm Rowe] asked me if I still wanted a change. His friend, the contractor, wanted a team and scoop hand. I said yes, but I was reassured that I could come back to the farm if I was not satisfied and anyway I could treat them as home at any time. Good people, I regretted leaving but the new job meant five pound a week. It entailed camping and roughing it. Food was included but the camp cook was no Mrs. Beeton. There were five other men in the camp. The cook for some unaccountable reason acted as a sort of work foreman. He was not a very nice character. He was another ugly Australian, a semi-alcoholic and very hard to get on with. I got off side with him right from the start. I was a total abstainer which meant I didn't join in his drinking bouts. I also found he didn't like overseas people. I trod warily because I was told in town he was a dirty brawler not averse to using any weapon at hand. There are always some drawbacks. I consoled myself that £5 a week was too good to have it spoiled by a pub brawler. I found out that he was some in-law relative to the Boss, so perhaps that was why he tolerated him.

I got farther into the black books when the Boss periodically chose me to go out on various one man jobs, because he said, I wouldn't be blind drunk on the job. I would have felt happier if he had kept the reasons to himself, but he had made it known in the camp probably as a rebuke to the drinkers.

We had three eight-horse teams in [for] the large wagons. We were carting gravel to surface the roads, which up till now had been formed earth tracks. Our haul was eight miles over fairly rough tracks. We had no earthmovers. We shoveled the gravel into the wagons after we had ripped the earth with a horse drawn plough. What a change today with all the mechanical equipment.

It was summertime and the sun was merciless, and that ubiquitous pest, the bush fly, nearly drove us mad at times. We loaded about six cubic yards in each wagon; the off-siders who came to help us with the loading were more often sozzled or working off a binge. I remember one sizzling day after loading I went to my waterbag only to find someone had emptied the lot. I had a burning thirst. On the way there was a dam, so we lined up and drank in bush style with our cupped hands. After drinking, I looked across the dam and saw two dead sheep floating in the water. Some of us went a bit green around the gills.

One of the teamsters was a youngster of my own age. Andy came from South Australia; we became good friends. Like myself, Andy was struggling to save enough to start on his own. He was a great little toiler and we helped each other. How insular some country people can be was brought to light with a local councilor who approached the Boss telling him he should not be employing Dagoes. When asked by the Boss where the Dagoes were, he indicated Andy and myself. Stripped to the waist and burned black by the sun, he mistook us for southern Europeans. Dago was a loose term for any southern European.

The Boss, [Mick Panowitz], bore a Polish name and most of the residents in the surrounding districts were of German ancestry. Like someone said of America, we were a melting pot of assimilation. We are now a pressure cooker. The post Second World War era saw a flood of migrants from war torn areas, though the primary reason for bringing them here was still cheap labour, to carry on with dirty jobs where it was hard to get labour. But the then Minister for Immigration, Mr. Arthur Calwell, had a wider conception of migration and set the stage for wider vision of what the whole business was about. Today we have thousands of young

Australians with names representing countries and peoples all over the world.

CHAPTER ELEVEN

We had finished one contract and were now engaged in re-surfacing a section of the Western Highway which was a main link to Adelaide. The work was harder as we had a shorter drag and we were now expected to deliver two loads a day which meant much more work loading. We were given an extra hand but that only meant that our other helpers eased up and took it easy. I had been taken away with my team to do some grading on another contract. When I came back the sub-foreman never let up, he was possibly jealous because the Boss relied too much on me; anyhow, in the course of an argument he pulled a knife on me. But Andy and another chap intervened. Result was, Andy and I both packed up and headed for town. That evening, later, the Boss turned up at the pub where we had booked in, to get us to reconsider. I said no, and Andy decided to head for home, and we arranged to meet in Horsham for the new year.

I had a suit being made at the tailors, so I had to hang around for a few days. I got a job helping a chap to put in rifle butts for the local rifle club. A word here for the hotel keeper; I had booked in at mid-week, the tariff was reputed to be £1 a week for those who spent a bit in the bar or 25 shillings for tee-to-totalers like myself. At the weekend I asked the hotel keeper what I owed. He looked up my booking, then said leave it till the week is up, then it will be £1. Wanting to be honest I said, "You know I won't spend too much at the bar." "I know," he said, "where the hell would

I be if I spent too much at the bar?" They were good people. [Hotelier by name - Reg Butler].

I gave some thought to going back to my friends at the farm, but my pride said that it might seem that I had failed them. I did meet them a few years later. With my wait for the tailor finished, I headed for Horsham and to meet a friend Bill [Bill Kyle] who traveled with me on the Moreton Bay, and also Andy who didn't stay long as he had got a job near to home. Bill and I had our reunion and celebrated Christmas and New Year. I think that New Year's Eve was one of the liveliest I can remember. We danced in the streets of Horsham till morning, hundreds of young people enjoying a get together. (Bill married a young lady from Stawell but we lost contact.)

Main Street, Stawell, Victoria, about 1925

I was offered a job on a farm near Horsham, which I felt tempted to take as I had met a girl in town and we seemed to get along. However, I heard that a big bridge was going to be built in Sydney, and they were looking for men, so I decided to go there. An Englishman staying in Horsham was going to Sydney. We decided to travel together; he turned out to be disaster; I carried him. I lent him money and on our return to Victoria I helped him to get a job. He never repaid a cent and I found he was a wife deserter and a general no-hoper. He is one of the minutiae of my life I would like to expunge.

Sydney, I loved the place. But there was no work. I went to the Trades Hall there and they told me that Sydney was a mire of unemployment. As for the bridge, it was always a stunt of contractors to advertise, just to make sure they had labour when they wanted it. A pool of prospective employees was their insurance. I did the rounds of the employment agencies - nothing doing.

Now, when I left home, the boys who had come from Australia had given me lists of contacts around Sydney who could help me to get work. Again my stupid pride; I still wanted to do it my own way, so back to Victoria.

CHAPTER TWELVE

That decision to return to Victoria probably set the whole course of my life. I have sometimes regretted since that I had not chosen the northern states but then I may have missed my life's partner, and that would have been unthinkable.

Now during my unsettled period, I had no correspondence except from the young lady at Horsham. Arriving in Melbourne, I went to the P.O. where my mail was to be re-routed. There was no mail. But I was advised to inquire at the Dead Letter Department in the Bourke St. G.P.O. There I got several letters. It was apparent that the country P.O. was at fault and had ignored or mislaid my re-direction notice to Melbourne. Amongst the mail was a letter from my brother Jack, telling me he would be arriving in Melbourne from Ireland on a certain date. It was a red letter date which I can't now recall. Unfortunately, the date had passed while I was in Sydney. I was in a whirl of excitement. My brother was here somewhere in Victoria.

Jack was eighteen months my junior. We had thought to leave home together, but my father, exercising parental discretion, had decided it best that I try out first, and of course both of us being minors, we had to accept the position. Twenty-one was the age of maturity in those days, not eighteen as it stands today.

John J. (Jack) Kelly, was born on 25 February 1906 in Lisnafin, Co Tyrone, Ireland. He like Patrick emigrated from Ireland to Australia. The two brothers caught up with each other and at some point decided to try their hand at building a farm. (c. 1927)

Tragically Jack drowned sometime around October of 1930 while swimming in a lake formed by the building of a dam. This was near where their farm was to be located. Patrick had no heart or desire to continue this effort after his brother's untimely death. Patrick sold the farmland and moved from the area.

Now to find Jack. I had the address of the Migration Department; I went there. It was then situated in a fusty old building in Russell St. not far from Flinders St. the Migration people were really good. They went through the records and I found that my brother had gone to work on a dairy farm near Meeniyan in Gippsland. I caught the first available train to Meeniyan or maybe it was Dumbalk. What I most remember was a three-mile walk along a dusty road bordered by thick Ti-tree, out to the farm.

What a reunion. We talked all night. Jack's employers were a couple of bachelor Englishmen (Beatty and Antrobus) trying to make a go at dairying. They were most hospitable and invited me to stay as long as I liked. I spent the following day with Jack cutting bracken fern and blackberries. This was fill-in work between milking times on most Gippsland dairy farms in those days. As I have earlier stated, the mushrooming hills and sunshaded valleys of Gippsland tended to depress me. I wanted the open country and far horizon. I was at the moment out of a job and could possibly have found work on some nearby dairy farm, but linked with my aversion to Gippsland, I didn't like working with cows. Having been reared in a farm environment where cows were a seven-day a week chore, I decided that milking cows in Australia would be the last thing I would do. (I have over the years developed a love of bush country).

After hearing all the home news and events of his voyage, Jack and I started planning for the future. We decided that when he got a few pounds saved we would get together and take on some contract work. In retrospect one realizes how futile sometimes are the puny plans of men, but we could not see the future then.

I was driven to the rail station and so back to Melbourne and the debasing task of finding a job. There was nothing at the Government Labour Centre. Queues of men waiting. There were the private agencies where you had to pay. A list of jobs would be posted outside and a rush of men, who were generally seated around, would gather to peruse the notices. If you saw a job that you thought might suit, you went in and applied. Sometimes a prospective employer would have to be met; some of these characters were very arrogant and expected so much efficiency from an ordinary farm hand, it could have been thought they were going to pay an extravagant wage. Such was not the case. I met one such fellow. He wanted a windmill mechanic, farrier, butcher, and horse-breaker all for one pound a week.

I had made a fair hole in my savings on my trip to Sydney, but I wasn't broke and so was in some position to dictate what I expected from my employer. That is, of course, if workers are ever in a position to dictate anything.

I had decided on some sort of bush work where I could be my own Boss. There were a few options, like fencing, timber cutting, clearing scrub, etc., where a sort of contract was available. I might state here that there were traps for the unwary in some of these jobs. One had to first find out if the contract was not a sub-let job. In such set-ups, a contractor put in a price for a job, then let it out to someone at a lesser rate. Another pitfall was the danger of doing a certain job, then to find there was no money forthcoming. So it was pertinent that one question the bona fides of a lot of employers in the bush in those days. I recall a friend of mine who worked for twelve months for a farmer getting fobbed off with a dud cheque. There were many such incidents. One character used to send to the Bureau for a young fellow. When the employee lad would ask for an advance of pay, he would get a bashing and the sack. He met his match in a young Irishman who happened to be a skilled boxer. But that's another story.

CHAPTER THIRTEEN

I finally settled for a job on a eucalyptus plant, more because it gave me a chance to live in the bush. I loved the bush setting, I still do. The Englishman was still hanging on like the leech he was. He was broke so I had to foot the bill for our tools, etc. He was really an embarrassment, but I suppose I was softhearted in those days. He was a stray dog and I just couldn't turn him out.

The location of the place of work was a few hours train ride north from Melbourne, (Stawell district). It was an old mining district and steeped in mining history. The Grampian Mountains made a beautiful background for the surrounding bush country. Most of the cleared areas were given over to grazing. The Forest Commission also controlled treed areas. The country where we worked was pitted with old mining shafts and digger holes as we called them.

I don't think there is much of the industry existing today. It was the extraction of eucalyptus oil from the leaves of certain eucalyptus trees. The plant where the oil was extracted was a fairly crude but efficient set-up. There were two or three large concrete vats about twelve foot deep and eight foot across. The leaves were tumbled into the vats and trodden in with steam applied. A large concrete lid was lowered on by a crane. Steam supplied by a large boiler was pumped into the vats. The steam was emitted through pipes and a condenser. The effluence was thus drained to another tank and the oil separated.

The plant had originally been a gold processing plant, where gold in a fine state was recovered by a chemical process. A large water storage made it ideal for the eucalyptus project which was the effort by an enterprising man to wrest a living for his family from a fairly harsh environment. He was assisted by his brother who did all the carting. The project was now, we hoped, going to give us some sort of living too.

Well, there was nothing glamorous about the job. Our first months were spent in the forest and we slept in the open with a bed of leaves wedged between two cut logs and a bower of branches formed into what the aborigines called a "mia mia." It didn't take me long to realize my workmate was hopeless as a bushman; if he hid his tools he couldn't find them again next morning. I remember when we had been there about a fortnight, we found there were two old fellows working about a mile further out in the bush. After work one evening, we decided to visit them. We had a good social evening playing cards and exchanging experiences. I found the family of one of the men's mother lived in my home district. They shared a good tent but like all old bushmen, they had a row occasionally and one would sleep out.

I'm diverting from the theme of my story, which was my mate's lack of bushcraft. It had been a nice moonlight, but by midnight on our return journey some clouds were about. I found the way back as I had broken a branch here and there on the way out. Coming near our camp I said to (we will call him "Hob"), "You go and light up and I'll pop over to the dam and make sure the camp fire is safe." On arriving back where we slept there was no sign of Hob. Well, I thought, he is probably in the Universal toilet, he will be in soon. I lit up and waited, minutes passed. I coo-eed. No reply. I got really worried then; the place was full of digger holes. I grabbed the lantern and headed out, calling all the time. I got to the old boys' camp and woke them up. We had three lanterns and headed out walking abreast, avoiding holes and yelling out. After some time we heard something thrashing about down in the valley; probably some cattle, one old boy said. Then we heard a faint call. Sure enough, it was Hob; his clothes were in ribbons, scratches and cuts all over him. He had gone straight past our camp, walked around in a circle and panicked. The bush has a curious effect on some people, they become completely disoriented even in daylight. After Hob's episode, one of the old boys suggested I tie a cowbell on him.

I think I can fade Hob out of the picture now, though the partnership lasted for some months. He did some very nasty things to me, and never repaid me one penny of money I lent him. I was thereafter very wary in my choice of friends. The great Australian illusion of mateship has been blown many times by people like Hob.

CHAPTER FOURTEEN

In my ramblings, I have omitted to tell you what our job really was. To people not versed in the doings of the bush, I suppose some of this may sound like Bulldust. Well, our tools of trade were an axe and sickle, and we always kept a spare axe because even with the best intentions axe handles do break. Our job was to fell the trees and then lop off the leafy branches; these we would drag into a heap, if possible, in the shade of one tree we would save for that purpose. Then with the sickle we cut the leaves off leaving twigs of wood no thicker than a finger. These we would later load onto the wagon pulled by three horses. We got three pounds for a vat. So every time a wagon load went off we knew there was three pounds in the bank. Our main worry was when we got ahead of the carter and would have perhaps a hundred pounds worth on the ground, that a bushfire could go through. Summertime was the main worry time.

Our drinking water was always brought out by the carter. We got our rough water for bathing, washing, etc., from a dam. Sometimes I used to set a can of dam water overnight with Epsom salts to clarify it, then boil it. I wonder how the youth of today would like the life. We had no way of keeping butter. Fresh meat was a problem, we didn't have a wire safe. But then I have seen maggots scraped off a leg of lamb and then had it served for dinner.

I remember often the delight of Mrs. M. when the carpenter made her a coolgardie. This was a cupboard-like frame covered with hessian, a dish or a tank full of water placed on top, and a piece of towel put on to the water and draped down the hessian sides. With a sort of capillary action, the water was dripped down the sides and with the wind action formed a cooling process. Water was always a problem in the Mallee. It was decided to use dam water. The dam water was unfiltered and when the mud saturated the hessian, poor Mrs. M.'s jellies and custards came out a lovely brown. I could write a book on the trials of a Mallee housewife in the early 1900's. In later years I was to make a coolgardie for Doreen and it was used successfully until replaced by an up-to-date ice chest. Even the then modern ice chest is now a relic and the once flourishing ice-making factories are now almost gone.

An old miner told me where to find good water in some of the mine shafts. We could lower a billy, weighted, on a long length of wire, till we reached water. Some of the holes were over an underground stream and the water was excellent. Another tip was to put meat or butter in a hessian bag and lower it into the shaft. This kept it cool.

We found a tendency at first to drink a great deal of water. Axe work is strenuous and a thirsty job on a hot day, but too much water would make us sick. A good tip was to make a billy of black tea, put it into a couple of bottles and stick them into our heaps of fresh leaves with the open neck protruding; they would come out icy cold on the hottest day. I think some chemical reaction in the eucalyptus produced an ammonia. Not being interested in chemistry, I was satisfied with the ice cold tea.

One pleasure in the bush, which is sadly diminishing today, was the bird life. It was a treat to wake up in the morning to find flocks of parakeets, honey eaters, and the rosellas perched in the trees around the camp. Then the carol of the magpies and the groups of kookaburras making merry round. When we first met the forest ranger, he was puzzled by small trees left standing and sometimes little clumps of trees. I explained to him that certain birds were nesting there and when the birds had gone we would clean up. Some of the territory we worked had been cut over before and the new growth was more suitable for our purpose. We had to leave selected saplings for a future forest. I believe those times spent on that job were the most enjoyable of my working life. The sweet, clean smell of the bush and the fact that we could work our own hours and knock off when we chose...in the hot weather we used to start very early then knock off during the heat of the day.

Of course the job was no bonanza. I knew many chaps tried it and couldn't make enough to pay their store bills, and some never did. Thinking of store bills, I had broken partnership with Hob and my pay packet was much better. In our partnership I had paid all the store bills and other expenses, then sharing equal what was left. The store was run by two dear old ladies, and we ran our account until such time as our cheque came along. Some time after Hob was on his own, the store lady asked me about him and how his credit stood. I told her truthfully that he owed me a fair bit of money that I didn't expect to get. The warning didn't sink in, because some time later Hob did a flit owing a large deal at the store and another at the hotel in town where he had been living it up. Lucky for me I had notified the hotel keeper not to accept any credit in my name unless I gave authority for it. The hotel was used by me sometimes when I was in town overnight. Exit Hob.

The wet came and I moved in closer to the plant, securing an old deserted miner's house. The other two old cutters moved in with me. One later moved out into the bush again. His place was taken by another younger fellow. After talking to the Boss, it was decided that I write to my brother and ask him to come and join me. Jack duly arrived and a very good working partnership ensued. Not long after Jack arrived, we got news that brother Dan was on his way to Australia. I don't recall the exact date that Dan arrived in Melbourne, but it was Winter 1927. It was very cold in Melbourne and Jack and I had to invest in new overcoats.

CHAPTER FIFTEEN

Dan had been sponsored under a scheme called "Little Brother Movement". He was 15 1/2, about six feet tall and quite grown up since the last time I had seen him. He was accompanied by another chap whom I had known slightly at home. His name was Peter [Clarke], and he was staying in Melbourne while Dan was traveling on to N.S.W. where he went to an agricultural school at Yanco. On the face of it, the scheme may have seemed benevolent; it was in fact just another plan to ensure a pool of workers for the farmers and graziers. Australian employers have been adept at this business; when the source from Britain and Ireland started to dry up, an unlimited supply was found in Italy, later in Turkey. The Italians, however, didn't like working for a Boss, and banded together to acquire their own bits of land. The English and Irish migrants of later years had gained a feeling for independence and believed strongly in Trade Union protection. There is a fear that perhaps the next source will be from the deprived people of Asia. At the moment of writing, the employers and their appointed government seem obsessed with what is known as Union Bashing.

Lest it be thought that I am overly engrossed in this quota of my life, perhaps I am, it is a period I recall most vividly, as then it was that I first met my life's partner. With the free and easy work pattern of the job I was able to have more time for social life. I loved dancing and it was at a

Dulcie Sarah Redenbach was born on 27 May 1904. Her parents were, Charles Augustus Redenbach (1864 – 1923) and Sarah Violet McKenzie Redenbach (1877 – 1952). (c. 1927)

Carnival Ball that I met the girl who became my wife; after that meeting all other attachments became secondary. She had come from the city to visit a friend and have a quiet holiday. She found a job and stayed on. We were both twenty-three and mature enough to realize we were meant for each other.

Prior to this meeting, Jack and I had considered going up to Alice Springs where a rail project was in progress. Our names were registered with the contractors but it was not until the hot wet season came that we were asked to report. At this season a lot of the workers would leave because of the conditions. We decided that if seasoned men couldn't carry on, then it was not for us. The more likely reason on my part, I didn't want to be so far away from Doreen. We had been meeting, going to dances, and getting to know each other.

I still recall the Hall and the old silent pictures; there was a dance floor in front of the screen with raised seats at the back. Those who wanted to dance could still watch the picture and follow the script underneath. There was another picture house in the town but the old Paramount was our favourite.

I had some regrets then about an earlier decision. It had been the intention of jack and I to buy a car. Yes, even then a young fellow liked a car to take the girlfriend out, we were no different from today. Albeit the fact that we could have bought a new model Ford just out, for 240 pounds, we decided that the car would not be suitable to get to work in the bush. So instead we got a couple of pushbikes at £11 each. Many times later I wished we had bought that car. Just imagine the youth of today choosing a pushbike instead of a car.

Somewhere we had got some information about a land settlement scheme in Queensland, situated in the Dawson Valley. We had applied for consideration and had accepted. Later we were informed that we would each be allocated two small blocks of irrigable land and a tract of dry area. After talking it over with several people, we got all sorts of advice, mostly advising us that the place was in the Never Never, and telling us we would be mad to go there; with hindsight these people had never been away from the district they were born in. However, we contacted the government agency again telling them that we might not have sufficient capital. They replied that finance was secondary. What was needed was young men willing to work and with a desire to succeed.

After final consideration we gave the idea away. But I should state that at least in some small measure the early information by the Migration Department was being substantiated. The Queensland scheme was of course a state effort and was open to anyone and was not in any way connected with migration. In later years I found out that the battlers who survived the pioneer era of the scheme did succeed.

A new system had been arranged at the plant without our knowledge. Without going into detail, it would have meant more work for us with no increase in pay, or cash returns. Jack and I decided it was time to move on. About this time Doreen had to return home to the city because of illness in her family, so we arranged for a date and meeting in the city.

On a day in September 1979, I stood on the P.O. steps in Bourke St. and with a flash of memory, I relived the scene of 52 years ago!

CHAPTER SIXTEEN

It was a nice day; I can't recall the exact date. Bourke St. was crowded with shoppers. I looked up the street and there in the distance I saw her. At the same moment she must have spotted me; she started to hurry. My brother Jack was with me and after the first introduction, he vanished. There was so much to be talked about. Would I come soon and meet Mam? Well, neither of us had a job. I had some leads which would take me away from the City; this I did not want but I realized it was Buckley's chance to find work in Melbourne. Could I go to Mam's and leave some of my now surplus baggage? I had left some extras behind with the two old boys at the plant. For transport I had my trusty bike. Jack and I did the rounds of the labour agencies again. We were staying at the Peoples Palace in King St. In those days the Palace was a very good, well conducted place to stay, and a message could always be left for us.

Our good friends, the Forest Ranger, had given us an introduction to the Ranger in charge of Government Eucalyptus Project in Bendigo. As a fall back we paid a labour bureau for a job in that district on a Eucalyptus plant that turned out to be a fizzer. The job was a real take. On inquiry at the country store, we were told that men had been sent up regularly but no one stayed. The set-up was that the stores were supplied, but no money was ever forthcoming. And when anyone went looking for money, they got a bashing.

We went and had a look at the Plant and interviewed the bloke in charge. We didn't like what we saw and we couldn't get any straight answers. So we just moved on via our trusty bikes. Maybe they were as good as the Ford, they only needed muscle power to run. The Government Ranger was most apologetic but owing to the cut in Government Grants (does that sound familiar?) his own men were on short time, but keep in touch. Back in town we fronted the Agent who had sent us on a wild goose chase. We threatened to expose his racket to the *Truth Newspaper*. After some argument, he gave us our money back.

It was back to the daily round, get the *Age* early, read all the job ads, which if they were any good, were snapped up before they appeared in print. One lurk used by people who had a contact inside was to hang around, and for an inducement, get the inside information which was later flogged to easy seekers of work.

We had a nasty incident. Jack had been sent out to what had seemed to be a dud job, and he returned to the Agency and asked for his money back. He was refused and told to get out. Jack was a mite hot-headed and didn't like to be made a fool of. In a momentary spurt of anger, he reached over the counter and grabbed the Agent by the collar and hauled him up on the counter. The half-strangled Agent yelled to his off-sider, "Get the police." There were about thirty men milling around the office. One chap yelled, "You send for the police here and you won't have a bloody office to stand in." Jack got his money back.

I was working on an Agent who happened to be a countryman from Northern Ireland. I had been told that he was open to a bit of inducement; I told him what I wanted, a job within reasonable distance of the city, preferably market garden or orchard. It would be worth £5 or perhaps less according to what wage the job paid. I suppose £5 then would be like fifty today. Of course, the Agent got it both ways, the prospective employer paid too. Result was I got sent to a job within twelve miles of Melbourne. (Templestowe). It was an orchard approximately 200 acres. The wage was £2 a week and keep, with a fairly comfortable hut as living quarters. There was also some regulation of hours but there was no pay for overtime.

It was a bit hard after the free and easy life in the bush, and our own choice of when we worked. Still it was a job. About this time I had considered bringing my father and young sister to Australia. Earlier I had a setback; I had nominated my elder sister and found work for her. At the last moment she made a hasty marriage and canceled out. I lost some money on the deal but it was her decision. I pondered the wisdom of my father selling up and uprooting himself from his native home. Older people generally find it harder to resettle. The economic climate was then getting worse, so on second thoughts, we advised Dad to stay put. It was a hard decision but as events turned out a wise one. Though he lived to be well over eighty years, I never got to see my father.

Out of the blue, I had a letter from my first employer, Mr. M. telling me he had sold out in the Mallee and had bought a large property in

Western N.S.W., would I come back to help them? As an inducement, horse power on the farm had been transferred to a tractor. Under other circumstances, I certainly would have gone as I had a close affinity to the family, but no way now was I going hundreds of miles away from Doreen.

Jack had no job, I showed him the letter, would he like to give it a try? I didn't see that it would matter to Mr. M., Jack was a better worker than I was. Jack said, "I'll give it a go." I wrote to Mr. M. telling him of the plan. He expressed some disappointment when Jack got there. I suppose the family had got used to me. It was very unlikely that Jack would run away with one of the daughters; he was a very shy man.

CHAPTER SEVENTEEN

I settled in well on the orchard, much of the work was similar to what I was used to, in the earlier days on the farm. I had started work when I was twelve so had good apprenticeship. There was only one worry, how was I ever going to save enough on £2 a week for Doreen and I to set up a home? Had I been aware of it then, there were a lot of couples trying to rear a family on less than that. The storm clouds of the Great Depression were hovering but hadn't quite broken then. I had saved a little bank account in the bush. We talked things over, and we didn't have much idea of the cost of running a home, but one thing was sure, we would set up a home.

Providence sometimes deals us surprises when we least expect them. I had openly discussed my problem with my employer, he was a good old battler with a large family. It's true he had a lot of land which at today's values would be a bonanza, in fact much of it today is covered with stately homes, but in those days money was tight. Many times a load of fruit, after diligent packing and carting to market would be brought back and dumped in the horse paddock or given to some charitable institution on the way home. Whatever some people may think, fruit doesn't just grow. There is tillage, pruning, spraying, manuring and picking. Then after all the gentle care, a wind or hail storm may come up over night and smash tons of fruit to the ground. I've seen it all. So knowing all the difficulties, I didn't expect any favourable reception to my suggestion that perhaps I could have some increase on my modest £2 a week. "It wasn't possible just then, when did we think of getting married?" It would be wishful thinking to name a date, say next week, next year maybe. We were not getting any younger. There would have to be a house to think of, furniture, etc. It was a big problem.

"Well," the old Boss said, "you know the number two orchard, there's a good little empty house on there. There's plenty of fire wood down on the creek. It would be loaded on the cart now and again and then left near the house. At the moment there's only rain water tanks, but the rumour is that the B. of W. will put water through soon. If that suits you, I can add that to your £2. Why not call it a deal and make your wedding plans." I knew he wasn't exactly playing Father Christmas. Number two orchard was two miles from the home block and did need someone in the house to protect the fruit in season from marauders. I was also aware I was a fairly efficient orchard hand. The house was not bringing in any revenue. Taking everything into account, he was on a winner. Was I looking a gift horse in the mouth? There was no gamble but, you know maybe a little of my birth place (Glasgow) rubbed off on me, but then I wasn't a canny Scot, I was a canny Irish-Australian who badly wanted a lovely Australian girl to share her life with him.

I told Doreen of the proposition. We looked at everything. We even tried to pry into the future. Well, only God knows that. Who knows, perhaps He was up there guiding us. We worked out what would be the necessary requirements for two people to found a home. Oh, we knew that countless generations had faced the same problems. Our needs would be basic: a bed, some chairs, a table, crockery and linen, a wardrobe and dresser. What a list. I thought back to my first shack in the Mallee, then the mia mia, just a mug, plate, camp oven, two kerosene tins and cutlery for one. What a lot extra two people need. Floor coverings, luckily there was lino on the floors. What a long way we have come with all the electrical gadgets, washing machines, (my grandmother-in-law used to have a field day washing in the creeks) electrical cookers, T.V., radios, carpets wall to wall...What - o - the good old days!

Can it be that I am a chronic rambler? I keep getting sidetracked from the business in mind. I was recording our plans for marriage. Well, we gradually picked out and put on lay-by the things we needed; it was great fun on late shopping nights. Doreen was working, she had not gone back to her trade of dress making as it affected her health. She had some nursing experience, so she got a job as a companion to an elderly lady. We had no difficulty planning our meets to go shopping. We had taken no one into our confidence about our intentions, after all it was our business and ours only. We were not really secretive people, but mum had a young family on her hands and we didn't want her to be burdened with the worries of a wedding and the cost it would entail, just to entertain a lot of people who mostly wouldn't be seen again anyway; so we went quietly on our way. Imagine our surprise, we had just finished our lay-by on a double bed when we were hailed by one of Doreen's girl cousins who wanted to know what was going on. I'm not sure if we swore her to secrecy, but she never let us down.

I kept in touch with Dan's travel mate Peter [Clarke]; he was working in the Mallee, so I wrote and booked him as Best Man. Peter [Clarke] agreed and turned up at the appointed time. We remained life long friends and he was known as Uncle Peter by our family. We enlisted Doreen's sister who was not quite eighteen to be bridesmaid, and on Boxing Day 1928, (December 26th) after Mass at St. Mary's, Thornbury, we were married...I made my haven and found the dear one who was my life's partner.

* * * * * *

BOOK THREE
The Romance years

BOOK THREE

An' I am rich because my eyes have seen
The lovelight in the eyes of my Doreen.
An' I am blessed because my feet have trod
A land whose fields reflect the smile of God.

~ Adapted from Dennis ~

God grant me the serenity
to accept the things
I cannot change,
And courage to change
the things I can,
And the Wisdom
to know the difference.

* * * * * *

CHAPTER ONE

Boxing Day 1928, after Mass at St. Mary's, Thornbury, we were married. A few sightseers remained to see the wedding. One lady was called to be a witness because Cis [Claire] was too young to sign the register. That lady became a dear friend and like a mother to us.

We had arranged for a quiet wedding dinner. After dinner we went to see Mam, then off to Luna Park for the afternoon. Some people may scorn and say what a paltry way to celebrate a wedding. We were happy and unlike some swank weddings that I have known, ours survived fifty years of stress and struggle without ever a harsh moment.

Let me reiterate, it's not flash weddings or extended honeymoon tours that make a marriage. It is the honest intent of two people who care for each other, and who are willing to concede that each have rights that must be respected. I can honestly say that for fifty years we lived for each other. Of such are good marriages made.

There is, and secretly has been, one nagging regret and that was about Mam, as I have stated, we thought it was for her welfare not to have her worry about things. In retrospect, I'm certain we should have included her in our plans. I lost my mother when I was eighteen and Mam was my second mother. I loved her. She came from pioneer stock of English, Irish and Scotch ancestry. Her parents had gone into the wilderness to have a home when they married and Mam knew what a hard life was.

Wedding photo of: L – R, Peter Clarke (Best man), Claire Redenbach (Maid of Honor), Dulcie Redenbach Kelly (Bride) and Patrick Kelly (Groom).

On Boxing Day (December 26), 1928, at St. Mary's Church in Thornbury, Patrick Kelly and Dulcie (Doreen) Redenbach swore their oath of fidelity to each other. One lady was called to be a witness because Claire was too young to sign the register.

==

Of ancestry my children have now inherited Scotch, English, German and a dash of Irish blood which goes back into the mists of history...fairly representative of what is known today as the Dinky Di Aussie.

We arrived at our little abode by taxi at midnight. I was almost too tired to carry Doreen over the threshold. I got a bit hot under the collar when the Boss knocked on the door the next morning to see if I was going to help them pick apples. I was uncivil!

Not long after our marriage, Jack had arrived back in Victoria. Well, he now had a home to come to. I got him a job in a neighbouring orchard. He admired Doreen. His first visit to town resulted in a present for us of a nice bedroom suite. It did the rounds of the family for many years.

We still had a hankering to get a few acres, and things seemed to work out for us. My employer, whom I shall call Mr. Will [Jenkins - family still own store in Scoresby], had bought 200 acres of bushland with intention of planting a new orchard, because he said the present land would some day be subdivided. It is today mostly built on. Adjoining the 200 acres was another fifty which we acquired. It was virgin bush; our plan was that I keep working for Mr. Will and weekends, I would try to clear enough to make a start. We would put some sort of shelter on it and live there while Jack kept on working and gave us some money for subsistence. Well, may man plan. We saw not the future.

Our first born, a girl, arrived at the end of October 1929. Doreen had a bad time, and for the babe, poor little thing, she fought strongly for existence. Doreen couldn't feed her, and after repeated food trials which baby rejected, we settled on an imported compound which was satisfactory but it cost 12/- a week which made a hole in our £2. I had to go away to a new place (Seville) which was forty miles away, so Doreen went up to stay with Mam.

We had cleared twenty acres of the two hundred timber, and with the aid of two horses and a large single furrow plough, I broke it up. We planted cherries and plums which were a disaster. Rabbits and wallabies made a playground of the clearing. I had, with use of axe, mattock and tree puller, gradually cleared a few acres of our block but it was a long way from being productive.

About this time Doreen decided we should be together. Now the only shelter was a small tin hut with a chimney of green saplings. Furniture was two bush stretchers made with hessian back, stretched on two bush poles and the usual Kero boxes for seating. I had managed to make a reasonable table out of bush wood. This served also as cupboard and repository for our meagre cooking utensils including a camp oven.

To this pioneer abode, Doreen came. True to her pioneering ancestors, she settled in. She stripped bark from the stringy bark trees and plaited mugs. She also indulged in sketching bush scenes which she loved. I made a bush crib for Bab. We were happy. It was a Saturday afternoon. I went down to our block; Doreen was following on. Bab was now starting to take a few steps. I came to a large ugly gum tree which I had decided was too much labour to grub, so I thought I would ring bark it and let it die a natural death. The ringbark operation meant making a frill incision round the tree deep through the cambium tissue. This stopped the flow of sap and the tree would eventually die.

Lest it be thought we were hell bent on destroying all trees, not so. We sought to have a balance of shelter belts and cultivation. I have always believed in conservation.

I suppose I was preoccupied, and without taking the usual precaution of checking above, I plunged the axe into the tree. I must have dislodged a needle sharp dry spar. It rocketed to the ground just making a cut in my shirt and opening a wound in my shoulder; just a few inches and it would have pierced my brain. I was badly shaken when I thought my wife may have found me dead. I didn't want to alarm her but she saw the blood. I brushed it off by saying I must have scratched it. After some healing ointment and a bandage we declared it a bush holiday. Could that have been an omen of things to come?

CHAPTER TWO

Start of October and again the weekend. It was like a burst of summer. I was stripping some stringy bark for Doreen who was making a carry crib for Bab. A car pulled up with Mr. Will and his wife. I thought, that's unusual, she doesn't often travel much. She came to me and I sensed something was wrong. It was Jack. His clothes had been found by a dam on the property where he worked. They feared he was drowned. No man should be ashamed of expressing grief, part of my world had just collapsed. I was completely distraught. We were ever close. Somehow Mr. Will drove us home. I was with the party on Sunday morning when Jack's body was recovered.

Recapitulation. Well, Jack's job was to market fruit. On Friday night he had gone to market; Saturday morning he had come home and turned his horses out. I knew he intended seeing a football final. There was a burst of hot weather. Presumably Jack decided to go for a dip. I knew he had suffered as a boy from rheumatic fever; the dam was a former quarry with steep sides. If his heart was affected there was no easy way out.

Jack was laid to rest in Faulkner. Life had to go on. I had my wife and child. I developed an aberration. I could no longer consider going back to our - what was to be - Happy Valley. I wanted to leave the district altogether, but that needed careful consideration. My family came first. However, the matter was decided for us a few months later.

Mr. Will struck a financial crisis and told me he could no longer afford to pay me. We could live in the house free for keeping an eye on the orchard. Had it not been for the earlier circumstances I would probably have accepted the offer but I now hated the district, so we went and put in a few days at Mam's until we found somewhere to live. We had managed to stow away a few pounds, so we decided on a house rather than rooms. Children were not welcome in rooms or flats. We found a nice cottage. (Thornbury). The owner told us he had not received any rent from tenants in the previous twelve months. I gave him a promise, the day we couldn't see our way clear to pay rent, we would get out. So our little store of furniture was moved in. The urgent requirement was to find a job. It was only then that we realized the clouds of depression had burst and were rendering their fury.

It was inevitable that Australia would suffer effects from a slump that was world-wide, but being a young country with unlimited future potential, it should not have been allowed to drift.

The rot set in under what was then the National Party Government. I think I'm being correct about the party's name - it has been changed so often. To me they have just been the Conservatives. Under the leadership of a man named Bruce, aided by a C.P. man named Page, cutbacks were made in government finance. The Commonwealth line of shipping was sold (good-bye old Moreton Bay). The Navy was put in mothballs, the most of Army regulars were put on reserve, the Airforce was allowed to deteriorate, Government contracts were slashed. Results of all this, thousands of men were thrown on the labour market. There was no money, was the cry.

(During the War a fiduciary issue was made of 10/- notes without gold backing. **For WAR**?) When a proposal was made to issue extra money, a howl rose from the money brokers - "Inflation"- that word maybe rings a bell!

Maybe students of History will see a parallel in the setup of nearly fifty years later. Late in 1929, the Bruce Government was tossed out and Bruce lost his seat. This is not a political chronicle, but I have always held Bruce and Page responsible as the architects of nine cruel years of misery and despair. I say cruel because even though there was full realization of the sufferings of thousands of people, no effort was made for early relief.

The first tottering efforts were in the nature of charity handouts in the form of food coupons. Later an inadequate payment known as the "dole" was made. It was only when the ranks of the unemployed were swollen by what we now know as white collar workers and bankrupt business men, most rendered inoperable by the Government tardiness in settling up for work contracts. Farmers were walking off their farms in the hundreds. The business men with probably better brains than their blue collar mates started to organize. The Government retaliated by starting relief works such as forestry and land reclamation. Men who gave too much trouble in their own district were hoisted off to some outlandish place where they could not organize. Refusal to accept meant being struck off the register. Human nature being what it is, many little petty tyrants sprang up. Put behind an employment counter and vested with a little authority, they were little Napoleons. It took no mean courage to stand up to some of them. Being wiped off the relief register in many cases meant a woman and child would go hungry.

I was so saddened and sickened by some of the things I knew of, I prayed to God that I would never accept their foul charity. I worked on relief jobs, yes, but I never took a dole. I am not expecting any haloes for this stance but I had said I hadn't traveled twelve thousand miles to be treated like a pauper. I wanted work and the right to rear my family with dignity. It breaks me sometimes now when I see the same situation being invited. I pray to God for my grandchildren.

The Government following Bruce did no better; they were hamstrung by foreign investors who had poured money into the country in the early twenties. Capitalism is, of course, a conglomerate, there's no heart to break, no bottom to kick, and like the cuckoo when the eggs are laid, can head for other fields.

Depression 1930 - 1980

When ruin and desolation walk the land,
And strong men weep and tell their fears to God,
Around them the wastes of Mammon's planning
For desolation thrives where man has trod.
When pompous lackeys steeped in financial guile,

Well versed in schemes meant to enthrall
Spread forth their plans for quick enrichment,
It may seem ruin for us all.

History's pages repeat oppression
And today we see again
Men sell their souls to acquire riches
Oblivious of their brothers' pain.
Is there hope that we may gather Wisdom
In our tenure of this earth,
And learn to share with one another
And recognize each other's worth?

"No, No" This idea was born in Dreamland
A proposition quite unsound,
Just a financier's nightmare
Let it rest where fantasies abound.
Let there be no talk of human equation
In our Bible Might is right,
In our Gospel, God is Mammon,
Him we serve with all our might.

Yet for all man's strict conjuring
And wealth on paper to confound,
And e'en though gold and diamonds are enduring
Not thus shall happiness be found.
For Mammon's pillars are firmed in ashes,
Abide not the strength sublime,
And like men and earthly scheming,
Wealth is just the Guest of Time.

~ P.K. 1982 ~

CHAPTER THREE

Following our shift into the suburbs, I vainly tried to work near to home; the chance was Buckley's. So, with Doreen's young brother, I went off about 200 miles north to cut wood for a woodyard. (Sandmount). The contract was so much rate against a rail truck of sawn wood. It was a hopeless setup, but they say drowning men clutch at straws. We had hoped. The timber stand had been cut over many times and the carters robbed us by always taking a load for their own use. The camp conditions were primitive. We tried hard but had to give in and head back to town. (General Store in Port Melbourne). Our little fund was dwindling. I had a letter from friend Peter [Clarke] enclosing part refund on a loan I had made. It was Heaven sent. Peter was up in the potato country and hoping to do a spot of spud picking. If I came up, I could bunk in with him and a mate and have a scout around; I might land something. It was almost eighty miles uphill, but I packed a couple of rugs and hung the old billy on the bike and away. (Fern Hill, East Trentham).

It seemed there was never going to be any home life. My baby was at an interesting stage, maybe she would forget me. The strain was worse on Doreen. Friends said, why don't you knuckle, go on the dole and don't worry. Sometimes Pride is a hard master. Stubborness and Pride are not traits to merit praise. My mother used to say I was stubborn like the legs of the donkey.

It was nearly dark. I had traveled the district all day. Nobody seemed anxious to start a digger. There had been some rain, the ground was wet and inspectors didn't like wet spuds to be bagged. I was heading for where I thought my camp was. I was hailed by a couple of fellows at a camp fire...an old Irishman and his son, "We have just had the evening meal - have you eaten?" It struck me then that I hadn't eaten since the previous evening. It was rabbit stew; never did anything taste so good. I felt fit to take on an army. They were just waiting for the ground to dry a bit. Did I have any luck? No, well, try old so and so about a mile away. I didn't waste any time. The old boy was a bit grumpy. As a matter of truth he wasn't all that much older than me. "Have you done any digging?" I considered. I was an Irishman, I said, "does it differ much here?" He said, "you are home, it's all Irish around here." Well, I guess spuds are spuds no matter where they are grown. While I was never a great spud eater, I reckon they taste good straight from the soil and one can never really starve while there is a paddock of spuds handy. Below are a couple of recipes from the spud diggers cook book.

White Stone Soup - Serve Two

Take a white stone about the size of a cricket ball. Wash stone carefully. Place in saucepan with four cups of water. Add one or two teaspoons of salt. Bring to boil. If thin soup is required, remove the stone.

Irish Potch in the Bush

Take one elephant's foot. Clean thoroughly. Three large potatoes. Wash clean. Have red hot fire. Place foot on the coals with potatoes. Bake 1/2 hour. Foot will probably melt, but potatoes are tasty. Same can be made with the front legs of two chickens.

A story which used to go the rounds which was symptomatic of the times - a couple of chaps were humping bluey down in the western district. They were passing by a farmyard with a lot of geese fussing around. Geese or ducks it was said, are very partial to a nice piece of meat dangled along on a hook at the end of a line. A gander had just swallowed the bait when a farmlady came out. The boys started to run with the gander, neck outstretched and wings flapping, dragged behind. The lady called out - don't be frightened boys, he always carries on like that.

There was no glamour in spud digging; it was a muscle searing, back breaking slog. I soon discovered that the style of digging that I had been brought up to would not do for contract digging. In my early training, it was considered a mortal sin to miss any tubers; I soon found my fowl scratching style didn't make for many bags per day. I speeded up. I would never be a gun digger but I was better than average. I remember a young chap came up to me one day and asked me how it was going, which meant what was I earning per day. I said I got to go like blue Hell to get 15/-. That would not have been bad had the weather permitted work for six days every week, but on an average we were lucky to get seven days a fortnight.

I looked the young fellow over. He was just a stripling. He said, "if I can't average £1 a day, it's no good to me." What I didn't know then, he was a gun digger reared on a spud farm. He made his £1 a day! Gun diggers are a very select club - or I should say were. The potato digger of today mounted on his traction powered machine wouldn't know a spud fork from a broom.

On a wet weekend when I knew I couldn't work, I would hop on the bike and do the 80 miles home to Doreen and our Bab. I would head off Sunday afternoon for the long push back. I recall one such return journey. I busted the bike chain about 25 miles from camp. I decided on a short cut through a forest track. I used to coast down the hills and walk on the flats. Dark came down. There was some moonlight; I was on top of a hill and coasting down. I thought I was nearing a main highway; it turned out to be a stream swollen with rain. Having no brakes, I went in up to the waist. Later I struck the rail line which I followed, and finished my journey longing for a cup of tea. It was past midnight when I reached the camp, and my cupboard was bare. My room-mates had been on a huge binge over the weekend and cleaned up the larder. "Oh, for the days of the Kerry dancing."

One nasty incident remains in my mind. When I was not going home, I used to send Doreen some money early in the week. Money was not easy to come by. My employer was often short of it too until he got a cheque from the potato agent. Anyhow, we scratched up £2 which I enclosed. I didn't have any spare cash to register it after buying a stamp, but the postmistress, whom I knew, assured me it would be all right. (Northcote P. O.). Imagine my horror; I got a note on Friday to say no money had arrived. I saw the Boss and he borrowed a couple of pounds from the Pub. So, I got on my bike and headed for Melbourne in time to get weekend supplies. I made several inquiries and lodged a written complaint. I never got my £2 but a month or so later a mailman was trapped for stealing from letters.

CHAPTER FOUR

Doreen was expecting again. She wanted to be with me. I advised against it, but she arrived. The friendly families around made her very welcome. We got a house with some furnishings. Baby was well afoot by this time. We had a heavy snowfall and it was a fairy land for Doreen, who had never seen snow before. No work could be done, but I had laid in a plenteous supply of logs.

There was a little runt of an Irishman camped with Peter [Clarke] and I before Doreen came up. That's where you meet all sorts of characters - at the spud digging. This little bloke claimed to be a seaman and used to regale us with his exploits during the Trouble in Ireland. His only claim to fame, with us, was his capacity for grog. The little bloke, we will call him Tom, had been hitting it pretty hard at the Pub. A latecomer entering the Pub was nearly knocked over by a rush of men leaving the Bar. The Pub keeper reckoned that Tom had reached the limit and told him he was barred. Maybe the slate was at the limit too. According to the only witness to stand his ground, Tom produced a pistol from his pocket and aimed it at the Pub keeper. He missed but shattered a large bottle of whisky on the display shelf.

Some Good Samaritan rushed Tom back to the camp. I, being the sober one, coaxed the pistol from him. It was an old single shot of Belgian origin. It was full of fluff and dust and Tom had held it too close to his nose when he fired. I dropped the pistol down the trunk of a hollow tree. The Hotel man was a good Irish man and forgave a Patriot like Tom. Funny men the Irish.

I could write a book on the characters and doings in Spud Land. But forgetting that most of the inhabitants were of Irish origin, they were a fine hospitable people. Eventually the season ended. There was no further work but we had survived the winter. My two friends, Peter [Clarke] and Jim, had all ready hit the wallaby for the Riverina where they had a contract and hoped to get some work at the wheat harvest. I had decided to go there too. I had been offered to work the run down place where we had a house on a share system. One employer offered me all the seed I would need, another offered me his horses in return for putting in his half acre. But how to exist and keep a family; some of the share farmers were already on Government relief and one leading farmer had 1,000 bags rotting in the paddock because it didn't pay him to cart them to the rail. The bottom had fallen out of things with a vengeance. No it would have to be the high road for me again. We needed hard cash, not a Kathleen Mavourneen.

I had a little purple patch. I got a bit of late digging in a nearby district (Fern Hill). It was good going. I had a cheque for £20 so I went into town to finalize our account at the grocers. Strangely, I had been able to get credit which was denied to some of the locals. The grocer looked at the cheque which wasn't a local bank "Oh," he said, "there will be sixpence exchange on this." "O.K.," I said, "there will be one and sixpence discount on my bill." That was the regular if I paid under thirty days. "My God," he said, "you are not an Irishman, you are a bloody Jew." "Well," I said, "seeing you had been so good to me, I was going to overlook it, had you not opened your mouth." "Fair enough," he said, "see you next year."

With the vagrancy of pregnancy diet, Doreen had got a craving for oranges which were a luxury. I got a half a dozen large ones, and a candy stick for Bab. There was still enough left to see us home.

It is no easy task recording from memory, and as I have to rely on a vibrant memory, it is possible that some events may be out of sequence, and for an easy flow, there may be some retrogression. For this I apologize, but it does not detract from the veracity of the Journal.

The old Pub was the social centre of the district. Not being insular as some country districts are, the locals and the blow-ins mixed easily. Where did the derelicts get all their drinking money? Well, there was always some farmer with spending money and after all it only cost a shilling to get started, and beer wasn't so dear in those days. Many of the characters were a circus in their own right. The young generation of today should not carry the can for drop-outs. They were there in my generation and in the one before and probably in the well regimented world of Julius Caesar.

Probably World War I and the Depression had caused an upheaval, but there was a proliferation (call them what you like) of drop-outs, derelicts, wanderers, the flotsam and jetsam of humanity. Many found rest for a while in that country Pub. There was the Count and Countess, an occasion decked out in what was once regal finery, even a top hat. They were camped out in the forest, probably Russians. There was old Mac, a skilled engineer, a rep. for Massey Harris when they first came from Canada to Australia, now an aged derelict. Big Jim, quoted as being in the Diplomatic Service in Ireland, sported a large red beard with his head shaved like an egg topped by a white pit helmet. He must have had a private income as he couldn't dig enough spuds to feed a pig.

Big Swede used to stand out in the rain with a spud bag over his shoulders, waiting for the sun to shine. Hans, the young German, who worked with me, used to eat his meagre supply of rations in a day, live on potatoes for the rest of the week. "Mein Gott, I'm hungry," he would tell me. He was always hungry. Kelly, who had been an architect in Sydney - downfall, booze - his main ambition - to crown Big Jack Land King of Australia. Old Pi Pi, a local pensioner, he was incontinent, but wouldn't leave the bar in case he missed a sound. He had a special spot near the door, and at times a stream would issue through the door on to the roadway.

Everybody knew Tom and his dog. Tom carried his belongings in a sugar bag and dog used to guard the swag while Tom wet his whistle which was often. One day was whizzed off with a drinking party. Like another famous dog, the little animal sat with the swag for nearly a week till Tom sobered up enough to come and get her. Tom was twitted one day about not going to Mass. "Oh, I'm a good Catholic," says Tom, "so is my dog.

She won't even eat meat on Friday." Oh yes? "Well, I'll bet you a quid," said Tom. Someone got a piece of meat from the pantry and laid it on the ground. The dog, well trained, advanced. Tom held up an admonishing finger - "Friday!" he said - the little dog slunk back and sat down. What most people didn't know, the dog's name was Friday. Queer characters. Then there was me. "He doesn't drink and he isn't Irish. Queer isn't he? Oh dear. What are the Irish coming to."

I have been back to that district not so long ago. It looked a lonely place. The old Pub still stands (was The Pig and Whistle) but all the old people are gone and the young are scattered. Land is mostly grazing, not much potato. Only the ghosts of those scruffy, queer, happy old diggers who have gone to that great paddock specially reserved for spud diggers. Vaya con Dios!

CHAPTER FIVE

I had intended to ride the bike home, but when I saw Doreen, Bab and the dog on the train and it looked like a storm, I blew the extra fare and went with them. Unfortunately, our bedding and baggage was mislaid and it was a week before it turned up. Doreen had given up the house when she had come to me, so we were back again to dear old Mam's. You know, she wasn't really old then, but I suppose the worry and care had aged her, but she was our sheet anchor.

I intended going to the harvest, but in the meantime I contacted a friend who had some influence in the Railway Dept. with some hope of employment. I got an interview and was offered to put in a month at my own expense, that is, without pay, as a trainee station assistant. I might then be eligible for casual work. To accept such an offer was, of course, impossible. About this time rail employees were on short time. I think it was three days a week for married men, and one and a half days for single men.

I was anxious to get work as soon as possible, so loaded again with the necessities for the road, with ten shillings in my pocket, I hit the road to travel 200 miles to the wheat lands. (Finley and Blighty N.S.W.). I remember getting to a section of the road called Pretty Sally. In those days it was a very steep section. It has now been regraded. On the way up I came upon a chap resting by the roadside. We traveled on together to the top where I decided I would sample a bit of lunch Mam had provided. We shared. He told me he had left his family in Brunswick and was on his way up to Bourke N.S.W. where his brother had a farm and he hoped to get some work. He had been in what he thought was a secure Government employment but got stood off. We parted, I on my bike, and he hoping for a lift.

I recall one later afternoon, I saw a dairy herd being milked, so I thought I'd buy some milk for tea. I was met by a burst of profanity. "No bloody milk!" I tried to explain that I was going to pay for it, but met with extreme rudeness. In trying to analyze the behaviour, I thought that maybe he thought that I was a Dairy Inspector or someone trying to trap him. I knew there were a lot of stupid laws pertaining to the sale of milk. But I reasoned he was just an ugly person and I would loved to have applied my fist to his nose. I got some milk in the next town. I didn't want to risk lighting a fire, so I came to a little house, apparently that of a railway employee. (Murchison East). I asked the lady if I could get some hot water. She said, "Will you come around and wait while the kettle boils?" It was tea time and a bevy of children was seated around the table. Just a happy family. Looking at me again, the mother said, "Why don't you have a bite of tea with us? It's only plain but you are welcome." After the dairyman, my faith in humans soared again. I thanked her but said I had to keep moving. I sat down to a lonely meal on the banks of the Broken River, and made my bed near a large ant hill. Bush lore says that snakes don't like ants and ants don't move around at night.

I was awakened by a road transport very early and rode into Shepparton with the dew still on me. I called on some relations, had a cup of tea and a rest and then on my way again. On my way towards the Murray, I thought the road director was pointed wrong. Three chaps were working nearby, so I asked them the way to Tocumwal. They pointed to the sign so I supposed it must be right. About three miles on, I saw a man on a tractor so I asked him. "No," he said, "you gotta go back to the cross roads." I told him about the fellows and the road sign. "Oh, that pack of Bastards, they need their heads cracked." Well, I was only one, I couldn't tackle them though I felt like it. I just rode past.

It was nightfall again and I was looking for a place to bed down. I saw a light shining through the trees. It was a little school house. I went into the yard and sitting at a fire was my traveler to Bourke; he had got a lift and had beat me to it. He spread his blanket on a play bench and said there was room for another. I said, "I think you will find that a bit hard. Just scoop a hole in the sand and you will be more comfortable." "I'm frightened of snakes," he said. However, some time after, he was on the ground – "too bloody hard there," he said. We parted next morning.

On the third day I arrived at the farm where Peter [Clarke] and Jim [Dudgeon] were already domiciled. (Finley - what used to be Tuppal Station). I was made welcome by the cocky, and the permission to bed down in the woolshed. To the uninitiated, a cocky is a slang word for an Australian farmer. My dictionary defines it as "wheat cocky," " bush cocky," "cow cocky," etc. I suppose our cocky would have used the prefix "sheep". "Anyhow," he said, "if you feel like giving a hand with the sheep to pass the time, that will be O.K. and don't forget where the dinner table is."

Getting an early start next morning, I was berated by Peter [Clarke] for waking them up so early. It's no use looking for work yet, they said, settle down. I said, "It's all right for you lazy buggers, I have a family to keep." So, I took the road. After the usual hiking around, I got a start. But I wasn't quite happy when I was told later that there might be some rubber cheques involved. I couldn't take the risk.

I moved out and was lucky to get another start straight away. My job was to top off the wheat bags and sew them up, then help the carter to load. I had done this work in the Mallee, so I had no worries. I think that old man was the fairest and most generous farmer I have known. It was close to Christmas, which is a time when families like to get together. My family was two hundred miles away and we were in the middle of harvest. The wheat season is a busy time. "No worry," they said. "Tell her to come up, we will meet the train." That's how it was with those kind family people. [Walter Cowan]. And as the story goes, so it came to pass, we all sat down to Christmas dinner. Doreen was delighted. One of the young men had journeyed into town and got a load of Christmas presents including a doll for Bab. They are all gone now, but may God be kind to them - true Christians with the spirit of Christmas.

Doreen was invited to stay on for some time. She was happy and gave some assistance to the lady of the house. [Mrs. Cowan]. Time came, she had to move on so I suggested she call on some relations in a large town in the Goulburn Valley [Shepparton] and try to find somewhere to live as the fruit picking season was my next hope. She soon wrote to me giving me our new address.

St. Brendan's Church, Shepparton, Victoria

Harvest was completed and I was on my way to the fruit land. I had received a five £ bonus over and above the wage we had agreed upon. Truly a gentleman. I intended riding all the way back but halfway I struck a severe thunderstorm and was lucky to get to a rail station where I caught a train and a surprise home coming.

On arriving at our address, I found it one little cramped room, but Doreen explained it was the best she could do. No one wanted children. Besides, there was a big influx of girls coming to work in the cannery - all needing accommodation.

CHAPTER SIX

Most people in the bush have heard of Tom Pepper, and the stories about him are many and varied, perhaps we could venture a little one - Tom at one time won some medals at the Olympics for prevarication. In fact, he was the world champion liar. Like all mortals, Tom died and joined the spirit world. He bowled up to St. Peter seeking admission. "Oh, no," Pete says, "we know all about you. You are a trouble maker and a liar. Try Nick down below." Tom fronted up to Nick's hideaway. "You can't come in here," Nick said. "See that big mountain over there? You can shift it down into the valley. That should keep you busy for about a thousand years." A thousand years later Tom approached Nick again. "I finished the job," he said. Nick pondered. "I don't like it down there, just shift it back again. That should keep you out of my hair for another thousand years." Another thousand years have gone. Tom is back again. "I don't know what I'm going to do with you," Nick says. "Well, I'm tired of shifting mountains, can I have a sit down job?" "Oh, yes," Nick replied. "You know that bridge over the river at Seymour? Well, you go down and plant yourself there till someone offers you a feed. That will be another thousand years."

Seymour, by the way, was known during the Depression days to the boys on the wallaby for its hospitality. They were met on the bridge by a policeman and escorted through the town to the junction of the Goulburn Valley Road about one mile out of town, and warned if they showed back in town they would end up in the caboose. We can vouch for the accuracy of this story as related by this fellow who was a direct descendant of Tom Pepper.

Back again on the wallaby. I was lucky at least to have the bike to get around. And again, I was a little different from some in that I did not want any hand outs. I was a labour hawker, all I wanted was a job, nothing to sell. I moved around the fruit district following up clues where someone was supposed to be putting on pickers. (Shepparton East). It was fairly grim. I stopped to talk with a fellow cutting brambles. We got to discussing the fruit scene, and he gained from me that I had worked in an orchard. After some discussion, I was about to move on. "Tell you what," he said. "We are not quite ready to start yet, but if you go down to the shed and see my foreman, I think he will find you something to do. It's good to get someone with experience." I had assumed that he was the labourer - instead, he was the owner.

I met the foreman, a little older than myself, an Englishman, [Ken Gray], and he started a friendship ending only with his demise a few years ago. We would start picking in a week's time - in the meantime there was plenty to do. The wage for picking was one shilling and threepence an hour, regular hours to be worked. I could grade and pack which was an asset.

As I got to know the foreman, I found he had been a victim of the Government plan of Navy Retrenchment. Aided by his young wife, he had pushed a pram and two young children with all their worldly possessions the hundred odd miles to this district. The orchardist had provided him with this job and a house. For that reason, he always dealt kindly to the boys on the wallaby.

Picking fruit is not exactly a job for weaklings, and many of the poor fellows were weak, their strength leeched by starvation or near starvation. Most were willing. Some had hiked or "jumped the rattler" from other states, all wanting work to preserve their dignity as men. I got to know many of them in ensuing years as an orchard foreman.

"Jumping the rattler," or free riding on the freight trains, was a means of long distance travel, but it was hazardous. The railway guards often boarded the trains and they did not deal kindly with the travel racked and often hungry youths. Some nasty situations often developed. One young fellow who picked with us had his leg almost severed. The answer of course would have been free travel vouchers for men looking for work but there was a complete lack of sympathy for the unfortunate. Even today in almost identical situations we find people with similar mentality. "Dole bludgers," and other similar remarks unthinkingly expressed by people who, only for God's grace, might be in similar circumstances. I have been there so I know.

Our boss and his foreman were not slave drivers so a happy rivalry ensued with the pickers. Being trained as a grader, I worked on the sorting tables set in the shade. There we sorted out what was suitable for canning.

The canning fruit was of a high standard and free from blemish. The second grades were packed for market, and the rejects taken away to be dumped.

Doreen's time was coming near. We had arranged for a private hospital in the suburbs where Mam lived. Something we ever regretted; Doreen and Bab went back to Mam's to be near her medical consultant. I was lonely without them.

The fruit harvest was in final days when one day I got an urgent call. I was wanted immediately. The call was from Mam. Things had gone wrong with Doreen. I told the Boss. He was very kind. "Just ring," he said, "if you want to come back to the district; I'll help you where I can." I was in a panic. There were no immediate trains to town and my old bike was feeling the strain - certainly not capable of the over 100 mile journey. "Call a cab" - that would be today's reaction, with complete ignorance of the financial family assets of those days. I went into town and went into a little cafe where the haulers used to pull up for a feed. A large truck pulled up. I recognized the driver as the man who had carted wheat. I told him my worry. "As soon as we have a bite to eat, we will be on our way," he said. That was the longest meal break I ever experienced. I thought they would never get going. My mind was going around in circles. I feared for Doreen. What was happening? Oh God, let it be all right. Let her be safe.

At last we were on our way. They wanted to hear what I had been doing. How was the fruit picking? Would I go back to the harvest next year? Keep in touch. They would look out for a job for me. It was like when Jack was lost. I couldn't think of anything but to get to that hospital. They were kind men and I think they just tried to cheer me and keep my mind off my worry. They dropped me off somewhere in Brunswick where I could get a bus across to Northcote. I offered to pay. The driver said, "Do you want a kick in the rear?" See you next harvest.

I got off the bus at Northcote. People looked as they saw me running along the street. Jogging hadn't been thought of then. I arrived at the hospital almost exhausted. Doreen was very feeble, but matron said she would be all right. I found that through medical incompetence the baby, a boy, had been killed at birth. It was only after a supreme effort by the very aged matron that Doreen survived. It was many months before she recovered her strength.

CHAPTER SEVEN

I strangely then didn't grieve for our lost son. In later years, however, I would look at the gap in the family and think what might have been. The effect on Doreen lasted longer than I realized, but I think it was something we agreed silently to leave in memory. When she was mobile again, we had to make a decision, battle it out on the dole in town or go back up the country again. One thing was certain, if Doreen wanted to stay, I stayed, no more separation. Finally, we decided the city atmosphere was palling a bit. The country town was a nice place and we had made friends. We would go back. In the interval in the city, I had borrowed a bike and rode out to see old Mr. Will and the family. Like everyone in their position, they were just keeping their heads above water; they were pleased to see me.

While in town, I went about selling our land. With Jack's death, it had reverted to me. We had a big medical and hospital bill to meet (no medibank then). If the return from the land would clear that up, it would give us a breather. Later we found a buyer and paid our debts. Confirming our decision to return to the country, I rang the orchardist. (Then Captain Rule, in the War he had been Major Rule). Yes, he had a patch of orchard to grub out, at least that was a little prop till something else turned up.

Back in our adopted town again (Shepparton), we set about getting a house. I was getting some casual jobs, enough to keep the wolves at bay.

We found a house with a large block of land. What a godsend, I was able to start a garden. I had a supply of veggies for the home and was able to scrape a little extra from the sales. Winter time and fortune was with me. Through the good office of a friend (an Irish Priest), I was picked for a relief job. It was tough work, re-laying a railway line. The work was limited to six days a fortnight for a married man. Pay was about two pound for a week. After three months work you could be terminated. Well, I didn't mind, I could now see the winter over. The bulk of the men had families in the city; it must have been hell for them, working three days in the week with the boredom of hanging around in the spare days, and they had no chance of getting home.

On that job I worked with men from all walks of life, mostly from the city. It was hard seeing a middle-aged ex-bank manager trying to swing a pick. Men who had been in soft jobs in the Public Service, men who had been in their own business; it was heartbreaking. For chaps like myself, used to manual effort, it was just a job. But one felt for some fellows when they started on a cold frosty morning and the blisters on their chafed hands started to break. Sometime, somewhere, someone will have to give a reckoning for all that misery. Please God, don't ever let it happen again. Probably due to malnutrition and constant worry, I broke out in a massive attack of boils; the sap from handling the red gum sleepers infected some open wounds which became septic. I was admitted to (the) hospital where I spent about two weeks. When I got back on the job, I found that all the men with whom I had worked, had finished their term. So I was among another team of strangers. My term soon ended and once again I was unemployed.

Some medic after Doreen's tragic loss, had said she should not have any more children. We talked it over. Well, if that is God's will. But, I thought in any case, some more medical advice was needed. So we went to see a sound old G.P. (Dr. Kennedy). After an examination and hearing our story, including the previous advice - "Bulldust," he said. He took Doreen's hand and said, "Look girl, you will never feel whole again until you have another child. So don't worry, I will take care of you." He was true to his word. When we had our second beautiful daughter, there was not the slightest trouble. Doreen was able to nurture her and with a new body to love, she forgot all her sad hangovers.

After my chore on the railway, I was again doing the rounds. I picked tomatoes, I picked tobacco, I cut timber, I done a bit of coal carting to the gas works for a local carrier, I done some concrete work. I did anything that would return me a shilling and keep me off the dole. Sometimes I fell for a job where the bloke would say, "I'm a bit short now, I'll see you next week." He invariably did, but I learned to pick my marks. That was how it was, you won a few, you lost a few.

The years rolled on. I had a steady job, with poor pay (£2 weekly) but it was regular, so long as I was fit to work. I was classed as the foreman on an orchard. It was when I had an injury that I again realized how little protection the worker had. Worker's compensation was a pittance. It was in the late fifties that any remedial action in this field was taken. There was no wage award available to the rural workers. We tried, with the aid of an A.W.U. organizer, to get some sort of cover for orchard workers. We met with frustration. Some of the orchard workers were working for their keep. Some were southern Europeans who were allowed shelter and the use of a small plot to grow veggies. Some were just retainers and thought the feudal system still operated. All these things, coupled with the tardiness of the A.W.U. in making any application for coverage meant defeat. In fact, we found that money collected from us was being used to finance the shearers' battle.

On the 8th of April, 1937, we were blessed with twins, a boy and a girl. God had given us a bonus for our earlier loss. The strain on our finance was now at breaking point but there was nothing we could do to improve it. The Depression was still dragging on. We had to consider ourselves lucky to have some income. The existing wage rate had been cut to ribbons by Government edict, and there was always a man waiting to step into a fellow worker's shoes. Rent was a burden. We vacated our nice little home for a cheaper one in the country. It was a ghastly mistake. I had to cart water from the main channel. The land where I was supposed to grow veggies was arid and I could not get water for irrigation when I needed it. The small iron roofed cottage was like a furnace in summer and with lack of insulation, was an ice box in winter. Through it all, Doreen never once complained.

For eighteen months, I struggled sixteen miles to work every day. The old bike had succumbed after long faithful service. A new Malvern Star bought on time payment didn't make sixteen miles any shorter. The twins, who Jonahs said wouldn't survive, thrived. The two girls were going to school. We moved back into town, it was a relief.

CHAPTER EIGHT

Can I fill in with a little levity? This happened at the fruit picking. We were picking apricots; a new man had started. He didn't look cut out to be a fruit picker. He was shaped like a large balloon on legs. His tummy was inclined to push him off the picking ladder; we called him Roly Poly. Roly was balanced on top of a high ladder. He lost his balance and grabbed hold of part of a tree which crashed on top of him. The Boss ran up. "Is the ladder all right?" he said. Then pointing at Roly, who was limping around after being assisted from under the tree limbs, "Look at him," he said, "not only has he ruined two cases of fruit, he has ruined a tree that took me twenty years to grow!" It's nice to get our priorities right.

It was maybe Shakespeare who wrote, "A little nonsense now and then is relished by the best of men." If I err, what the hell, Shakespeare has been credited with a lot of things that he never wrote. So no matter.

A fellow we knew was working a bullock team carting logs in the forest. This day he was driving along see, when the wagon suddenly stopped. Looking around he saw a large Goanna jammed through his back wheels. The bullocks couldn't shift the wagon, so he unhooked them, then twitched a piece of wire around the Goanna's tail, hooked the bullocks to him and pulled him out. Stooping to pick up his whip, he heard a scuffle and there was the Goanna up a tree with ten bullocks hanging head down from his tail. Queer denizens in the Australian bush.

Well, we were back in town. Our other boy was born in June 1939. An ominous year, war clouds were hovering. I had been having a lot of ill health. Our old doctor told me I had absorbed too much lead from the orchard sprays. "Give it away," he said. Not quite so easy, but a row with my employer found me out of a job. It was probably a culmination of events. My bouts of sickness, which probably soured my temper and continual requests for extra work without any rise in pay. My family obligations had increased and sometimes I had been doing the work of two men which didn't appear to be recognized by my employer, who I suppose like all employers, was taking advantage of the economic situation. Anyhow, early one morning after a blistering row, I packed up. It wasn't a happy ending to eleven years of hard work.

I dreaded going home to tell Doreen that I had no job. "Oh," she said, "I got a fright, I thought you were ill. Don't worry, if the worst comes maybe I can get work." What a partner. I felt so proud of her. No nagging, no carping, she restored my courage. Peter [Clarke], our old friend, was doing a bit of wood-cutting for a wood merchant. It meant camping out, but if I saw the woodman, he would probably give me a go. "No trouble," the woodman said, "but it's only a tucker job you know, not much out of it to feed a family." Well, if it was only a fill job... "O.K.," he said, "I'll cart whatever you cut right away." But, I never went to the bush. On the way from the woodyard, I met a contractor I had known from the early years. I asked how work was. "Oh, I can get plenty of men," he said, "but they are not much use in my job." He was roadbuilding. "Can you handle a scoop team?" I said yes, and told him I had worked on roadwork. "Oh, good," he said, "I'm going out on a job now. Tell me where you live and I'll let you know." We were again out of town about three miles.

Later that evening the contractor called. I could get a job but the job was thirty miles away (Benalla) and I'd be away from home and I'd have to batch. The wage would be double what I had received on the orchard. I looked at Doreen and she nodded. "Right," he said, "you have your gear ready and I'll pick you up in the morning."

The years seemed to slip away and I was back on the old job (road) of my earlier days. (Nhill). Driving the grader, working the scoop teams and pegging out. They were a good bunch of fellows. Had it not been for continuous stomach and chest pains, I would have been happy. The Boss called every weekend and took me home and someone would come for me again on Sunday night.

Eventually that contract finished and we were to move further out. I had only been engaged to replace a man who had broken his arm, but the Boss told me now he would like me to stay on. It was a good proposition but I didn't like Doreen and the children being on their own, besides, a neighbouring orchardist wanted me to help him in the fruit season. My old Boss had called on me and asked me to come back, but I said I didn't think he would want to pay me the money I now expected. I spent the season with the neighbour, a very good employer. In fact, since it became known that I left my old employer, I had received several offers. Bearing in mind, what my doctor had advised, I kept my options open.

CHAPTER NINE

In September 1939, the Second World War was unleashed. Prime Minister Menzies promised Britain our assistance in their struggle. Lots of men and boys I knew enlisted, and boys who had never known a steady job. With a short training they were off to the Middle East. "Five bob a day tourists," they were called. "Five bob a day" that was the magnificent bounty they received for risking their lives. A few short months before they had been nobodies living or existing on a pittance. Then wonder of wonders, somebody found there had been stacks of money there all the while. Just as if someone had burst a balloon of sovereigns, the money gushed forth. New training camps were built, new munitions works were started. Contracts on a cost plus system were the order of the day. All this after nine years of human misery because some blundering politicians had made believe there was no money. The profiteers were now set for another harvest.

Then came a bit of a lull, the war was nearly over. The Maginot Line was impregnable. The Germans don't want to fight Britain. What a lot of Bulldust. It was just as well, there was a lull because Australia was totally defenseless, thanks to machinations of Bruce and Page. We had no air defense, the first rush of enlistments were handed out, the moldy relics of the 1914-1918 war. Old 303 rifles, a danger to the user, were issued. We are not in much better state today in 1979.

When Japan came in against us later, our Airforce in their Wirraways and vintage planes went up to certain death. We left a battalion to rot in New Guinea because we had no Navy to evacuate them. One Prime Minister of the conservative ilk threw up his hands and said, "Let the Japs come in, we will keep them north of Brisbane." Some people wince now when the Brisbane line is mentioned. Nevertheless, the Japs have come in. Just check up on the record of Jap influence in Northern Australia today. It seems a lot of Australians died for nothing.

It remained for that shining light among all Australian politicians, John Curtin, to defy the great windbag, Churchill, and bring our troops from the Middle East to defend Australia. During this time of turmoil, we had left fruitland and all our friends. I had a job managing a grazing property. I suppose working caretaker would be a better term. I liked the work, my health improved. The home was primitive, especially with a young family, Doreen made the most of it. We were together. I think we spent about eighteen months there.

The war situation was now really serious. The Japs were pressing in on us. My conscience was nagging me. I had four brothers-in-law opposing the Japs some where in the northern islands. My young brother Dan was somewhere in the Middle East. I made some plans and enlisted in the R.A.A.F. My employer blocked me claiming I was in reserve occupation. I gave notice, sufficient time to allow my replacement. I asked Doreen to go down to Melbourne to try to find a home. She came back delighted; with the aid of her brother she had managed to pay a month's rent on a reasonable old home in a bayside suburb. We left the grazing property without regret.

Among the men who came back from the Middle East was my brother Dan. He had five days leave with his wife and two children. He now rests among thousands of his mates in Bomana Military Cemetery. They had met the Japs on what is known to history as the Kokoda Trail in New Guinea and stopped their push to Moresby at a cost.

L – R Irene Maud Rumage Kelly, Kevin, (Kevin died at the age of five), Valda May and Daniel Kelly. Daniel married Irene on 20 August 1932. They had two children Valda May, and Kevin. On 25 June 1940 Daniel enlisted in the military. Daniel was killed in action on October 28, 1942 in New Guinea on the infamous Kakoda Trail. He was first buried in (best read) Eora Ck Village, map reference 615766 Kakoda Area. Reburied Kakoda War Cemetery, Plot D Row A Grave 4, on June 4, 1943. (National Archives of Australia) (c. 1940)

Patrick Kelly (c. 1940)

==

I intended to forget the Airforce and join the army where I thought I might see some action sooner. At the recruiting office they told me I was too old. I was 37. Why should I want to join up anyway? Well, I didn't feel comfortable with my family relations carrying my burden. I got employment and joined the Home Guard or the Volunteer Defense as it was called. The war situation was getting worse. I volunteered again, this time I was accepted. Another barrier, I was again in a reserve occupation, but with a bit of persuasion I got a release. The reserve occupation was a bit of a joke. Large production companies wanting to be sure they had a pool of manpower, got protection from call up for their employees. It provided a haven for the section of the community who put self-interest first. A reflection showed that some of the companies who were harshest on the unemployed were now prepared to harbour on their payroll dozens of men doing practically nothing. Cost Plus contracts bore the costs.

I spent four years in the service, but I may as well have stayed in my job. I was mostly engaged driving heavy loading equipment. A recurrence of my earlier troubles barred me from service in the tropics. Our youngest child, a girl, was born in April 1945. Of my years in the service there was nothing very gratifying, but I often thought of the old saying - power corrupts. I've seen fellows vested with a couple of stripes become perfect little tyrants. I knocked promotion back three times, maybe for that reason, though I was trade grouped, which earned me a corporal's pay without the worry.

One thing sticks in my mind. Before I had my demob papers completed, I was sent to 115G Hospital. After several weeks there, I was returned to G.D.D. Royal Park for finalization of my demob. Somehow I got mixed up with a bunch on the parade ground. A corporal was throwing his weight about. Admitted that I was not very soldierly, having been in hospital and finishing anyway. My tunic was undone, I hadn't been worrying about parade drill. This little tyrant pounced on me. "Do that bloody tunic up. Smarten yourself up!" I was old enough to be his father. He gave me the rounds in front of the team. I said nothing; just then I heard my number called - 514728, report to the demob section. So, I walked off. When all the details were completed and with the little slip which made me a civilian, I undid my tunic, went over to the little bastard and said, "It would give me lot of pleasure if you would come down to the gate outside, so I can ram your bloody teeth down your neck!" No play. Only some haw-haws from the boys. And so my exit from the military forces. Oh yes, I have a bit of embossed paper which says that I served X number of days and no bad conduct marks.

I had forty days leave pay, but on contacting my pre-army employer, I was told to report as soon as possible, at least within a week because they were going to be busy. Early in the demob scene, the army had issued slop suits but this was discontinued. I had been armed with clothing coupons, (rationing was still in force). So here I was accompanied by Doreen, touring the city clothing shops trying to get some clobber which would make me look like a civilian again. There were hundreds like myself doing the rounds. "No hope," they would say, "nothing doing." But I was lucky and found a really decent tailored job, an order which hadn't been collected. It was a perfect fit. So I could now shed the last vestige of the army. It was like being reborn again. Doreen and I had some time for outings and had a chance to rediscover Melbourne again. We had spent many years in the country and Army life and the War had stifled any celebrations.

CHAPTER TEN

Fifty years ago, my Melbourne was just like a big bustling country town. That atmosphere in later years has been gradually eliminated by get rich quick speculators. The city is not being allowed to age gracefully. Admitted, efforts are being made to retain what are left of the gracious old buildings and some work is being done to rejuvenate the moribund shopping aisles. Nostalgia, I have been told, is not a profitable exercise. Never look back, they say. My reply must be that a man without memories is like a tree without roots.

It may seem that the miasma of the Depression blinded me to all the beautiful things in Melbourne that I loved. Not so. Who would forget the evening walks through the beautiful Botanic Gardens, the pleasure boat trips on the Yarra, and farther afield, the boat trips across the bay to Sorrento. Memory may not serve me fully, but I think it was the Edina. There was the thrill of attending the Sydney based film premiere at the Capitol Theatre in Swanston St. The film was called, "Those Who Love." There was a beautiful orchestra which used to appear from the pit to the stage front on an elevating dais. The orchestra was later replaced by a Wurlitzer organ. Then there was the opening of the new State Theatre in Flinders St., with the roof lit up to look like the sky, and the indecent little figures looking down from the stage trimmings.

No doubt there were costlier places of entertainment and dining, but for the ordinary mortals, like Doreen and me, a good meal could be had for 1/3. That was a three course meal, with lashings of roast beef, or roast lamb, with proper roast potatoes and veggies. Stacks of bread and butter on each table. Repeats of tea or coffee as requested, with sweets from apple pie and real cream to choice fruit salads - all for 1/3. No half dried up greasy chips and sloppy urn tea like today. There were even cheaper and equally as good places, but my favourite was on the hill in Bourke St., not far from the P.O. It is gone now. Then there was a choice little haven up near Parliament House much frequented by the cabbies. A nice three course meal cost 1/-.

I can recall the opening of Coles Variety Store in Bourke St. Nothing over 2/6 was the catch cry. Wares were laid out on tables, according to a price range from 3d. to 2/6. Perhaps my use of the old coin system may be confusing in the jargon of today. I've never fully accepted the juggling with our imperial system. Then there were the dear noisy old clanging cable trams where a 2d. fare would take you a long way. Question my reasoning or wisdom if you will, but I would hope to see retained all the things that are worthwhile from our early days, winnowed free from the evil of wars, depression and greed.

In that I support all those who believe in conservation. While not now aligning with any political party, I could probably be nominated as a Christian Socialist. I reject the pseudo Liberals and their catch cry of free enterprise. The god of this religion called Free Enterprise is Profit. In the minds of those enmeshed in this religion, the appeasement of Profit in itself is not evil, but when coupled with Greed and Misuse of Power, then the well-being of humanity is endangered.

No Politics. Well, it's my story. Can't I at least record what I stand for? If by chance my great grandchildren may know that I even existed, then I think they should have some insight as to what sort of person they had for an ancestor....

Since I can never see your face,
And never shake you by the hand,
I send my soul through time and space
To greet you - you will understand.
~ Flicker ~

CHAPTER ELEVEN

Under an army edict, ex-army personnel could claim reinstatement in the jobs they left to enlist. I went back to the meatworks (Vestys, Footscray), not because I liked it, but the money was much better than I could expect in other employment. The work was fairly strenuous, working sometimes in temperatures well below zero. The glare from snow on the ice-bound ceilings caused eye strain, but there were never many undue illnesses, some heart strain perhaps for the older men. I don't suppose I was ever really happy there though I put in twenty years. Like the poet Burns, my heart was in the highlands via the wide open spaces.

> *So the days of my riding are over,*
> *The days of my tramping are done,*
> *I'm about as content as a rover*
> *Will ever be under the sun.*
> *~ Lawson ~*

However, I need money in the bank. That dread insecurity instilled by the Depression was a haunt for many years, so I settled in and the years went by. Dickens or Steinbeck could have written many volumes on the characters who infested the meatworks during my 25 years sojourn. Being a seasonal occupation, the personnel who went through in any twelve months was amazing. I was lucky to get a steady run. Being a reserve occupation during the war, it was a haven for the two bob boxers, footballers, bookies, horse trainers, and jockeys and all such who needed an alibi to dodge the military call up. When the war was over, these fellows drifted away to their more lucrative interests, leaving a nucleus of old fellows, skilled tradesmen too old to fit in elsewhere, and a smattering of well educated people, mostly the jetsam of the Depression years, all good mates.

There was a curious kind of camaraderie that I didn't ever find in the army. Truly a lot of the old fellows could have stepped right out of Dickens. Bill, alias "the Bower Bird," had put a nice ham in storage for Christmas. How to get it out past the watchman at the gate? Bill didn't have a full title to the ham. Bill turned up at the gate one evening at knock off time, with a small packing case under one arm. "What's in the box?" says the watchman. "It's a present for my mum," says Bill. "I must open it," says the watchman. He did. Out jumped a large tom cat. A week later, the same scene, the same watchman. "You are not going to mess it up again, are you?" says Bill. "It's taken me a whole week to catch him." "I'm afraid so," says the watchman. Out jumped the cat again. "Now you've done it," says Bill. "Me mother's not going to like this." A few days later, the same watchman. Bill fronts up again with his box. He presented it to the watchman. "Naw, on yer way!" he said. Mother got her ham.

I was traveling 25 miles each way every day to work. It was a killer but we had settled in down by the Bay. (Carrum). Our children were happy at school and had their background and friends. It wouldn't have been fair to uproot them for a home in the western suburbs. I worked overtime nights and weekends and with Doreen's careful handling, the little bank

Patrick and Dulcie's Children
L – R; John, Claire, Neal, Mary, Patricia. Missing from the photo is Josephine. A neighbor who was a photographer took the picture, at Carrum, Victoria. (c. 1940's)

===

account was starting to grow. My children were growing up but I hardly ever had time to enjoy them. I was gone before they were awake in the morning, and they were asleep again when I arrived home near midnight. Much time was wasted waiting for trains which sometimes never arrived. How I wished often that I had the old Ford.

About this time we got notice that the old home was to be sold. As an ex-serviceman I had protection from eviction under the Landlord and Tenants Act, but I assured the owner we would vacate as soon as humanly possible. There was no hope of raising finance to buy the old place. We decided to get a block of land and start a home and maybe live there as we completed it. Building regulations were a bit more humane in those days.

Through the good offices of a friend, I was able to get finance. We got a building block at a reasonable price. I drew up the plans under instructions from Doreen as to how a home should function. With the aid of our boys, reinforced by the little experience I had acquired as a bush carpenter, a start was made.

It was great when we had the stumps in and squared, with the timber lying ready to make the framework. I eased up on the overtime. We worked at weekends and holidays and, may I confess, we sometimes fractured the Sabbath. It was twelve months solid labour and it was not complete when we moved in, but it was ours and we worked hard to finish it. Only those, who with their own hands have built their home, will know the pride we felt in our achievement. It has stood the test of many years.

Sometime in those years I penned the lines...

For Dulcie Whose Pet Name was Doreen

Could I wind back the dial of time,
This is what I'd do,
I'd live again those magic hours
When first I met with you.
The fires of youth were burning bright
With adventures in our hearts,
When first we challenged life's young dreams
And vowed we'd never part.

No music was more entrancing
No stars did shine so bright
When we danced into each other's hearts

On that enchanted night.
Then we wandered in the moonlight
To a Fairyland we knew,
There we built our airy castles
As lovers like to do.

The strange sounds of the bushland
Were with us everywhere
And the scent of gums and wattle
Perfume the summer air.
Many years have passed since then
But the music haunts me still,
I loved you then, I love you now,
And I know I always will.

Let's not ring up the curtain please
Until the stage is set,
We will travel back in fantasy
To the place where we first met.
Then let us spin the dial again,
And keep the picture clear,
For it's love that makes the world go round
And you are always near.

It would be nice to relive those happy days,
When you and I were young,
But God's been good, there's no regrets,
So let our song be sung.
We have trained and stayed the distance
And until the race is run,
We will sit and count our blessings
until Someone says, "Well done."

~ P.K. ~

Perhaps with a little respect for a 75 year old, a little retrospection will be pardoned. The picture of a lady hangs in our home. I have previously mentioned Sarah [Jessep McKenzie]. She was a pioneer. She came to this country from England some time early in the 1800's. With her husband, she rode on horseback to the wilderness of the Australian bush to hew a home, where they raised a large family. Regretfully, Sarah left no records of those early days, except those passed on by her daughter, Sarah [McKenzie Redenbach], my mother-in-law, the Mam of our story. One little snippet stayed in my mind. Sarah, in the early days, had cordial relations with the bush aborigines. In later years, when the tribe was decimated, an occasional black nomad would appear. One such arrived one day, and coaxed Sarah into buying a bag of feathers, very good, make feather pillows. Sometime later, Sarah discovered a flock of ducks had disappeared. My dear wife's second name was Sarah, and now four generations later we have another Sarah. Of such has our Australian nation been built.

Dulcie's mother, Sarah Violet Redenbach McKenzie (1877 – 1952) was born in Sale, Victoria, Australia. (unknown date)

Patrick was very fond of his mother-in-law. Throughout the book he refers frequently to "Mam". He also wrote a beautiful poem to honor her memory.

My mother-in-law Violet Agnes

I salute you Violet
Dear friend of yesteryear
When worldly woes beset us
You were always near

You were my second mother
I treasured your advice and care
No stranger to the trials of life
Of which you had your share

Mentor of our wayward years
Your help was good and true
Now, when wrestling with a problem
I always think of you

God give you rest my mother
And keep your memory green
An example to all mothers
Your life has surely been

May your offspring in the womb of time
Remember you with pride
And when the final roll is called
May they muster by your side

Pat 2-91

Sarah Violet Agnes Redenbach
(Nee) McKenzie, born in Sale, Victoria, Australia
Parents: John and Sarah McKenzie

Dulcie's grandmother, Sarah Jessup McKenzie

To quote from Patrick's text; "Sarah was a pioneer. She came to this country [Australia] from England some time in the early 1800's. With her husband she rode on horseback to the wilderness of the bush to make a home and raise a family" (unknown date)

CHAPTER TWELVE

I am truly grateful that this great land was discovered. But I deplore the manner in which it was acquired. When the first white settlers came to this country, it was already peopled. They came not as guests which they should have, but as invaders and conquerors. Some historians today are resentful that the original inhabitants made things difficult for the first settlers. Surely, they had a right to defend their own country. The treatment of the native Australian, was and is today, a blot on our history.

Song of the Aborigine

Time! What is Time?
There is Dark. There is Light.
There are things of which my fathers talked,
From whence they came or who they are
I know not!
I am here! This land is mine by right!

The wise men of my fathers
Gave us laws by which to live,
They in turn had laws
From the One who put us here.
We walked, we slept,
We had our ordered ways.
We loved our land
And what it had to give.

And then they came, the Spoilers,
With their vagrant ways,

We are the dispossessed,
We who have forgotten
What they ever learned.
But the spirit of our fathers watch
We have Hope, the land remains,
The One who gave us life is still concerned.

~ P.K. ~

From My days in the Bush...

Old Tom camped with us in an old miner's shack in the bush. He had a terrific nostalgia for the good old days in Melbourne. He had a particular craving for crays or lobsters. "My Gosh," he would say, "we used to have some beauties at Young and Jacksons." He used to make our mouths water. Some friends arrived late one night from up near the Murray. They brought with them a large bucket of live Murray lobsters. Poor old Tom was asleep. Some wag slipped a large lobster in near Tom's feet and turned out the light. I heard a terrific scream and old Tom was dancing around. I wasn't in on the joke, so I said, "What's wrong?" "It's a bloody great lobster," Tom said, "It's got me by the toe." I said, "Shut up you silly old bastard, you are dreaming; it's probably one of those big ones from Young and Jacksons come to haunt you." In the darkness Tom had knocked over the bucket. When the light came on there were lobsters all over the place.

Fat we have grown upon this goodly soil,
A little while, be patient Lord and wait,
Tomorrow and tomorrow will we toil,
The shade is pleasing Lord, our task is great.
~ Dennis ~

* * * * * * *

Now I think there's a likeness twixt Peter's life and mine,
For he did a lot of tramping long ago in Palestine.
He was "Union" when the workers first began to organize,
And I'm glad that old St. Peter keeps the keys of Paradise.
~ Lawson ~

Well, I did my little bit in the Union. After the war there were a lot of loose ends to be tied up. Such things as Workers' Compensation, stability of employment, conditions of work, safety, etc., etc. The tasks were many. Our Union had come under radical control, which I did not agree with. So, I thought, it's no use belly aching about it, I must get in there and play my part. It meant much sacrifice and eat up much of my spare time.

My first attempt saw me on the Central Executive, and State Committee of Management, and later, Treasurer, and for many years State President, a trust of which I was proud. I have always felt a deep sense of gratitude to all those members throughout Victoria for the trust they placed in me. I did my best to live up to this trust until I resigned as President on my retirement. For service rendered, I was honoured with a Life

Membership. Small time, you might say; well, to each his appointed task,

and any task which protects the interests of humanity is a task worth doing.

> *This above all, to thine own self be true,*
> *And it must follow as the night and day,*
> *Thou canst not then be false to any man.*
> *~ Shakespeare ~*
> *from Hamlet*

CHAPTER THIRTEEN

In July 1978, I visited the land of my childhood for the first time in 53 years. It had always been my ambition to take Doreen to see the land of my fathers. But God ordained otherwise. In 24 hours I traversed the distance which took me six weeks in 1925.

What were my feelings about my first sight after 53 years? Well, honestly, I don't know. There were the roads I had trod, the fields I had played in as a little boy. I didn't feel any upsurge of emotion which some people say they feel on such an occasion. Not even my old home aroused any spark of feeling or affinity for what many people call the Homeland. Were it not for my kin there, the place would mean nothing.

What did arouse a deep sadness and searing loneliness were the missing dear ones of my own family and the many friends who had passed on. My father had died when he was 87 and lived always hoping that some of his boys would eventually come back. "Such is life."

My sisters and their families made me very welcome and I met nieces and nephews by the dozen. But of my old schoolmates, about six were left; of course, a few still exist in America, where I have many cousins.

I was in London, and like that faraway day in 1925, I was partially lost and feeling jaded. There was no friendly bobby to turn to now. They all do the rounds in patrol cars, if they do any at all. Anyhow, I was tired walking; in the distance I spotted a building with an Australian flag flying. Something familiar. I won't be dramatic and say my heart started thumping, but I knew here was my bond with home, and that home was thousands of miles away. The building was the N.S.W. Centre and they solved all my problems. Would I make another visit? Maybe....

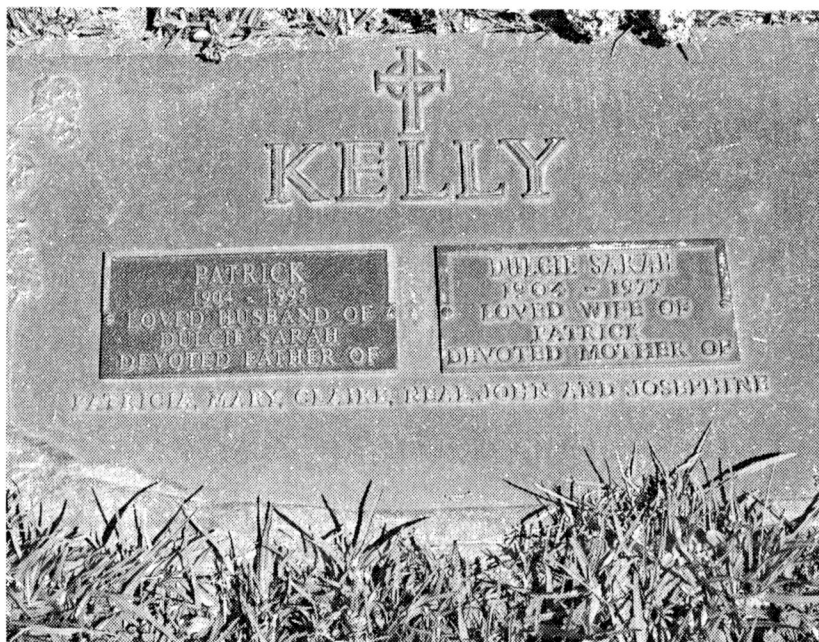

The grave of Patrick and Dulcie, located in Cheltenham Lawn Cemetery, Cheltenham, Victoria

An Irish Farewell

Farewell to the green fields of Gallon,
Farewell to the hills of Tyrone,
Farewell to my childhood companions,
Farewell to the friends I have known.
For tomorrow the party is over,
I'll be winging my way to the south.
After fifty long years of absence
I have seen the land of my youth.

Oh sure there were changes a plenty,
And many brave hearts they are still.
But there was no change in the welcome
When I reached the wee house on the hill.
One keeps on recalling the loved ones
And scenes that are etched in my mind
As I travel the long lane of memory
Seeing people that I left behind.

Once again I have walked around Sessiaugh
I have visited old Legfordrum,
I have ranged through the valleys of Gortin,
And rested a while at the Plum.
When Glennelly's quiet water is flowing,
There were scenes that I liked to recall,
And the streets of old Newtown Stewart
Well they haven't changed at all.

Now I'm thanking the Lord for his kindness
In allowing my dreams to come true,
And to all those dear people, my kindred,
May His blessings be showered on you.
Now all my dear friends and companions,
Once again we must part,

But whatever the future may harbour,
This "good-bye" will live in my heart.

~ P.K. ~
England 1978

Australia

Hail my adopted country!
Into the very inner recesses of my being
Your tendrils have entwined.
Land of ancient myths and truths
Land of contradictions,
Of burgeoning pastures and arid wastes
Land of burning sun and Alpine snows
You are the centre of my Universe.

El Dorado of the south
Ancient but forever young
Your ancient peoples ravished and dispersed
To them I apologize.

But I love their land
No cloying urge to own
Just the tenure of life
To live within its bounds
To climb its rugged mountains
Rove its wooded bushlands
Sleep beneath the stars
The Southern Cross my beacon.

And in the final slumber
Rest within its folds
The allure of golden sands on tranquil shores
Queen of the Southern Cross, Seduction is your name!
But honest is your lure
Prepared to give in full to those who seek.

For too long you have been ravaged by the spoiler,
All taken, naught returned,
Concrete laid, a substitute for grass,

Your streams fouled, and your earth laid bare,
Forests decimated to sate man's greed.
Weep not my beloved country
You have survived since the dawn of Time.
May the Creator who fosters all
Guard over you.
May the forests and rivers that have won my heart
Stand fast forever.
God bless Australia!

~ P.K. ~
May 1982

Deo Gratias - 1981

The magic years of youth have gone
And I am growing old.
I craved not worldly honours
And hankered not for gold.
For me the open spaces
And the quiet of the bush.
But many years I squandered
In the city's maddening rush.

When the years roll on and I am gone,
Please recall my simple plea,
To my kindred in the world of Time,
Just remember me.
Let me rest in the quiet bosom
Of the land I learnt to love,
Let no marble slab or concrete
Defile the grass above.

When morning sunshine bathes the land,
Well may my spirit stray,
To hear the magpie's morning carol
And scent the new mown hay.
Savour well while Time is long
God's blessings everywhere,
The birds, the flowers, the bushlands,
We are all meant to share.

~ P.K. ~

INDEX